THE DISPLACED CHUNKS OF MY LIFE

A Memoir

David Lawrence

ISBN: 978-93-6354-975-3

First Edition: 2024
Rs. 200/-

Cyberwit.net
HIG 45 Kaushambi Kunj, Kalindipuram
Allahabad - 211011 (U.P.) India
http://www.cyberwit.net
Tel: +(91) 9415091004
E-mail: info@cyberwit.net

Printed at VCORRE PRESS.

Table of Contents

Preface

My novel, *In the Suburb of Possible Suicide,* was published in February 2020 by Adelaide Publishers. *The Displaced Chunks of My Life: A Memoir* is a companion piece which is written as a subsequent memoir. Pieces are carved out of my ambitions. There is continuity in diversity. The stories and essays are subjectively true. The chunks of my life are independent and related. My life is as it is in separation and in the aggregate. It is fabulous and exciting.

These stories and essays are pieces of my life. I am a strange dude in that I encompass contradictions easily. I am a walking oxymoron. I don't care. I am comfortable in my dis-ease.

I was a professional athlete, an intellectual and a CEO of an insurance company. I was all this and all that. My careers spanned gulfs. I was written about in magazines and displayed on television shows.

I was thinking of writing a follow up novel to *In the Suburb of Possible Suicide* but I am an enemy of structure and prefer to examine the fragments of my life. I figure that non-fiction short stories would be much more managible for me. Afterall, I've been a poet for fifty years and I like the in and out quality of short structures. This book is novelistic in mood yet essayistic in structure. It captures my life experiences in fragments. Because it is non-fiction it is a memoir.

I don't make things up. Things make me up. I am manic. I am obsessed with myself and only want to write about my experiences. I am proudly narcissistic. I don't know other people. I only get a view into myself. I've led an interesting life. My stories are often more dramatic than fiction. I pick out different scenes from my life and put them together like patchwork. They are the book of my being. It seems to me that short stories have the brief structures of poems. Furthermore, they are much easier to understand than poems. Afterall, I've been writing poetry all of my life and although I have been published hundreds of times I have sold few copies of my books and my genius has been buried in the margins of disappearing graveyards. I am a newpaper blown in the wind onto a headstone.

About twenty years ago I gave a reading at a library where three people showed up. I figured something had to be done to get a bigger audience or make some money. I had recently been out of jail and only had a small stash of cash. So, through Gleason's Boxing Gym, I hooked myself up with some rappers and collaborated. This turned out to be easy in that I was a great lyricist and I could easily write rap lyrics.

In fact about ten years before this I wrote the lyrics for "Magic Man," an album by Sam Waymon (Nina Simon's brother.) It came out on Polygram Records in London. I flew to London to hear the opening and was impressed by myself. The BBC announced on the radio that I was a lyrical genius.

Well, after my jazz album I hooked up with Grand Master Melle Mel and the Furious Five. We did a few songs, one of them being, "The Wall Street Rapper." I also rapped a song, "I got a Hard-on Attitude" which the MC played as I walked down the aisle to fight Rodgriquz in Trump Plaza at Atlantic City.

But if truth be told I wasn't a very good rapper. I had no rhthym. The engineer in the studio had to punch me in and out. I was fabricated. I was not as fake as Millie Vanilli but I wasn't exactly real.

At the early beginning of my rap career I got caught for tax evasion. I did two years with the feds. When I got out I did a lot of rap songs, particularly, an album called the"Renegade Jew" which got some radio play and about which I did a video. I was flattered by the attention but I somehow didn't get many sales even though Funkmaster Flex played it on Hot 97.

I was deluded enough to think that the millions I lost in my failed insurance business would come back to me through my rap music. I made next to nothing. I don't know whether my distributer was stiffing me or not. I even was charted as number one in the dance clubs in the Midwest. I was ahead of Cypress Hill and Fat Joe. I had a following but no money.

I guess my rap songs were preparation for these stories. They were somewhat narrative and revealed bits of my life as complicated as it was.

When I first arrived at jail in 1993 I had paid for an ad in "Swing Magazine" and "Vibe." All the blacks in jail came up to me and said, "Yo. Are you the Renegade Jew?"

I knew I was safe. I was a rap hero in jail. Pretty cool for a middle aged, white, insurance broker Jew. Fortunately, the cons didn't know how much help I needed to stay on beat.

The Italians said, "Did we see you fight on Sean O'Grady's Tuesday Night Fights?"
"Knocked him out in the second round," I said. My stock went higher. I was the star of the Federal Prison Camp.

When I came out of jail my wife wanted me to give up rapping and boxing to move back in with her. How could I? I would have nothing left. I had lost my insurance company and all I had was the possibility of a rap carreer and enhancing my reputation in boxing.

So I had no choice but to move in with my parents and to teach boxing, do some modeling, do more rap songs and write books.

I ran through another hundred thousand dollars in the studio. I got a distributer, "Raging Bull Records," who put out *Lifestyles* by my group The Lost Trybe of Hip-Hop.

For promotions I went up to the Harlem Armory to box the famous rapper, Curtis Blow. I broke his ribs but we were in Harlem and they weren't going to give the fight to a white man. They announced that Curtis won but after that the promoters gave me a belt.

I never really made it as a rapper. Well, what did I expect? I wasn't musical and I had no sense of rhythm. I did some stand-up comedy at the major clubs. I got diagnosed as Bipolar and I went on lithium which tampered down my mania. I lost my interest in comedy and I stopped rap music. I went back to poetry which didn't cost me studio time.

A couple of poetry books that I published were *Lane Changes* (Four Way Books) and *Living on Madison Avenue* (Futurecycle Press.) I also published two memoirs *The King of White Collar Boxing* (Rain Mountain Press) and *On Jail*: *The Essays* (PrisonFoundation Press). They were not vanity press publications. They were real. I didn't have to pay for them. Still they brought in little or no profit because I didn't have a large book company behind me to promote my obviously interesting work.

I was brilliant but no one knew it. And although I had been a succcesful businessman I just couldn't bring myself to transfer my business instincts to poetry. Poetry was too sacred to me. I felt cheap promoting it.

In February 2020 my novel *In the Suburbs of Possible Suicide* was published. I originally wrote it as a film script in jail. At the Angelika Film Festival it was considered one of the outstanding manuscripts. Then I turned it into my novel which I was hoping would become a smash.

Unfortunately, when my novel came out in February 2020 the Covid-19 hit and
my publisher wasn't able to set up any readings. If my novel eventually works perhaps I can piggy back this book of short stories on it. I can make something of myself before I die. I can become my own legend. I feel I was meant to be part of the canon of literature. Why exist if not to be buried in the tomb of a book? Cover me up. Label me as "David Lawrence" in gold letters on the binder. Write me down on a card in the library.

I am almost famous. I am a short story that just goes on and on. I am manic. So what? My self-assessment may be grandiose but it is accurate. I am fabulous. Really, I kiss my own hand and don't even recognize that I am conceited. Everything I write ultimately comes back to me. I have no interest in understanding other people. They are protected by their skulls. I can't see inside of them. I don't want to know them. I embrace myself.

Pennies in the Sewer

Today is December 4th, 2019. I am seventy-two. Whoop, de do. I am obsessed with my approaching death and the possibility that I will lose my mind and kill myself. I doubt it. But then again I doubt that my doubt is a false signal. Maybe it is real and I am suicidal. I don't know who I am in the underbelly of the shark.

I usually don't bother to spend coins. I have five vases of pennies, nickels, dimes and quarters. I don't separate them. I'm not very neat. I don't roll them like I did as a kid. I don't count them. I just pile them in the jars and bags. I hate them. They have no value. They are meaningless.

I decide to gather a handful of pennies into a plastic bag. A few dimes and nickels creep in. I am not meticulous. It's a mess. I'm a mess. But I am a happy mess. I am a stone's throw from psychotic. I am jolly. I am manic. I am rarely depressive. I feel that sadness is a weakness. I am a man's man. Like my dad in World War II. I am the kind of man who doesn't give a *fuck*. Or I do and don't want to admit it. Or I do and I don't at the same time.

I don't fill the plastic bag to the top. I am worried that it will be too heavy or that it will spill. I like to leave some empty space in the bag. I don't like completion. When I grew up I would leave pieces of steak on my plate. To finish food was to be a pig. I liked being thin. But I don't want pennies to spill from my bag onto the street. I am worried that the cops will catch me and throw me back in jail for destroying money. Is that a crime? What do I know? When I caught a two year federal bid for money laundering I didn't even know that I was breaking the law. When you are driving in the street and go through a red light you are breaking the law. That is defined. I never know what I am doing. Am I illegal or within the confines of *juris prudence*? Who knows? Who cares?

I sneak out of the apartment on Madison Avenue. My wife is still asleep. She doesn't wake til one. She is a night owl. She stays up late playing on her I-phone.

I don't have an I-phone. I bought one at Verizon but couldn't figure how to use it. I was helpless. I returned it and got my money back. I told the sales girl that I was 72 and brain damaged from boxing so that I couldn't figure the phone out.

The elevator man, Ron, welcomes me into the wooden cabin. He is a year older than me and moves like a snail. He is always reading books and we call him "Professor." I feel closer to him than my rich neighbors. I lost my insurance business twenty-seven years ago when I went to jail for tax evasion. I am close to broke. The apartment is my wife's. At this stage of my life I earn less than the doormen but the apartment is my wife's and I only have to worry about the maintenance. It was worth millions but it isn't in my name.

Ron asks me what I have in the plastic bag. I tell him, "Pennies from heaven."
He smiles, thinking I am talking some obscure nonsense as I always do. He is from Guyana. He doesn't know much about Fred Astaire and Ginger Rogers in the movie "Let's Face the Music and Dance." He opens the door for me and recedes back into the lobby. I am not sure whether to drop the bag of pennies on the north corner of Seventy-Second and Madison or the south corner. I am too lazy to go down to Seventy-First. I am wondering if the cops will get the fingerprints off the pennies and come up and arrest me. I doubt that it is a major enough crime for them to come up with their guns in their hands like they did at my Wall Street office when they busted me for tax evasion years ago. There were twenty of them. I wasn't scared. I figured that wouldn't shoot me for tax debt. And I almost didn't care if they did.

I decide to settle for the Seventy-First Street corner in front of Ralph Lauren. I place the plastic bag filled with pennies in the bottom of the can. I feel relieved. Like my room will be tidier without the pennies. I feel like I am hurting myself by giving up something. The hurt feels good. My whole life I would occasionally punch myself in the face just to feel the pain. I like to give back to the God of pennies. I am an atheist with some stubbon streak of spirituality in my gut. When I was in my thirties I spent two thousand dollars on cocaine and flushed it down the toilet just to hurt my finances so that I wouldn't buy cocaine again. It worked. I never snorted another line. I believe in teaching myself tough lessons.

I walk down to the F train on 64th and Lexington. I think about when I was seven years old and used to play the sewer game in East Meadow. There was a big sump with a sewer on the curb on Linda Drive. That was about five houses from mine.
I would steal a bunch of pennies from my mother's closet. I'd walk down to the sewer and throw the pennies in. I felt free. I felt I could fly above money and material concerns. I never counted the pennies. I was not a perfectionist. I believed in giving back to the vast inexperience of life's naïve emotions.
And I liked to hurt myself. Years ago at Birchwood Summer Lake Camp I tried to show the other kids how tough I was by rubbing poison ivy on my face. A few days later I went to the nurse who told me that I had the worst case of poison ivy she had ever seen. For some reason I liked to do bad things to myself. It was romantic. It was the other side of a happy face.

In East Meadow my neighbor Steve in East Meadow came up to me at the sewer and asked me what I was doing.

I told him,"I'm feeding the sewer."

"Why?"

"It's hungry," I said. I sort of anthropomorphized the sewer and it became my friend. Sometimes you take things in by throwing them out. It didn't make sense. Pennies are cents. So maybe it made cents. The sewers were hungry.

Now I take the F train to York street in Brooklyn. I am on my way to Gleason's Gym where I had boxed for thirty years. I want to be punished. I want to be punched in the face. But I can't . I have brain damage from pro fighting and my neurologist advised me not to get hit in the head.

Getting hurt is giving back to the absent Gods. Life is about trading. Sometimes you lost, sometimes you won and sometimes you lost when you won and won when you lost.

I like myself. I am smart. I am the future of my sad, confused aging. And since then I have dropped occasional pennies in the street. I want to keep in touch with my sacrifices.

The Party and After at the St. Regis

It was Saturday morning, a day I taught boxing early at Gleason's Gym and then came home tired as a mouse at four o'clock p.m. and crawled onto my couch to take a nap. I was tired from sparring with a couple of my students. I am seventy-two, skip to my lou, worn out like a department store rug.

At seven o'clock P.M. my wife woke me from a nap and told me we have to go to a party.

"I'm tired, hon," I said.

"We'll only have to stay ten minutes. I'm calling a Communicar and he'll wait for us while we hop into the party and out," my wife said.

"Do I have to dress up? I'm not wearing a suit and tie."

"No, no, no. It's a disco party. Just wear jeans and your black velvet jacket."

"I'll do it," I said. I wasn't happy. I don't like to go to parties or mix with other people. As I get older, I become more of a loner. But I wanted my wife to be happy. She was all that I had left after I had abandoned travel, parties and general socializing. My life congealed. She was my past and my future. She was all I had to look forward to as I carried her from my past to my future.

I got dressed in five minutes. I even ran a comb through my hair. That was unusual. I liked messy hair. It made me feel young like when I was young and I wore my hair curly and sandy at the beach.

We went downstairs and the Communicar car service was waiting for us. My wife thought we were still rich. I rode the subways. She dressed in Oscar de la Renta. I wore the Gap or J. Crew, on sale.

Nice driver from Serbia. Polite. Reminded me of the days when I had a chauffeur driven Rolls Royce, backed up by two car services. My Rolls like was a traveling apartment. It was spacious and I felt protected inside of it.

My wife gave the driver the address. I wasn't listening. I never listen. I just think that anything anybody but myself has to say isn't that important. I suppose that I am a narcissist. I regard that as a compliment rather than a negative. Examining oneself is knowing oneself. The directions are an aside. They are relevant towards distance but not towards self-knowledge. What do I care about destination? I am my destination. I want to get inside myself and follow all the routes to vague self-knowledge. I don't look outside of the window. I look in the rear view window.

I am never really going anywhere but back into myself. I am my destination. I am going towards death. We all are. I go where I am. The world is a bore. Ho hum. I admire the Englishmen. They have good manners. They are more proper than Americans. They have Waspy behavior. They are not hiphop clowns who wear low slung jeans. Americans are disgusting and follow hip hop instead of opera. I hate opera. But I hate hip hop too. Despite the fact that I am a rapper. I do hate rappers. Imagine men wearing their pants low so they can show their ugly asses. What are they thinking?

It turns out that my wife gave the driver the wrong address. The driver looked it up on his GPS and we found it. It was on the twenty-fifth floor of some skyscraper and was some sort of party for its own presentation. It was Prince changing his name to a symbol. It was made up for the moment. It was something to do.

It was hiding from the possibility of something important. I hate parties. Almost as much as parades. I am outside the crowd looking in with closed eyes.

I knew I wouldn't stay long. I love people individually but hate them in groups.
My wife told the driver, "We'll be back in ten minutes." Sweeter words I've never heard.

My wife introduced me to some people who I forgot the minute I met them. She said I had met them before. What do I know? I am a cigarette break. I am here today, gone tomorrow. I am my wife's lipstick marks on my cup of coffee.

I grabbed some sushi off trays floating by on waiters' palms and cheered up a bit. Not that I wasn't cheery. I didn't know what I was eating. I never did. Sushi was sushi. Who cares whether it was salmon or fluke? But crowds betrayed me like isolated cruel remarks. I didn't want to be touched. Keep your elbows to yourselves.

True to her word, my wife said let's go. I said goodbye to people I didn't know and disappeared into an unfamiliar New York that had reincarnated its sixties hippy period into a liberal pandemic of bend-over-backwards, accepting, millennial, repetitive views.

I didn't know if we were going home or not. My wife told the driver to take us to the St. Regis. When we got there, she let him go. We couldn't afford to have him waiting around anymore.

"I love their salmon," she said.

"Tks for getting me out of there so early," I said.

"I'll even contribute twenty dollars to my dinner," My wife said.

That was so unusual. So sweet. Maybe she was beginning to understand that we were no longer what we were and to protect what we still had. When I lost my millions I could no longer float on waves of bric- a- brac and trivia.

I dove into my failure and pulled the air hose from my diving suit. But my wife rose above the squid and octopus and became a beautiful sailing vessel on the seven seas. She maintained herself as upper class regardless of our finances.

Our regular waiters weren't there because we usually came on Sunday afternoons. The place was fairly deserted. I hate crowded restaurants. I hate crowded crowds. And we were happy to get our favorite table, the first table on the left.

I usually order tea sandwiches but because it was eight-thirty at night I had to order the hamburger sliders. I love sliders but I prefer the dainty display of tea sandwiches. Still, the sliders were good. Just a little greasy like a low class person trying to articulate his simple thoughts. I also ordered a Bloody Mary sans spice. Of course it came with spice and I had to send it back. It takes a lot for me to send something back but I hate spice.

My wife ordered her grilled salmon which she had recently discovered there and loves. We chatted like we were Adam and Eve in Eden trying to make small talk about being naked. I looked at her and loved her. We had crossed so many deserts together. We were voyagers on the road to death.

After about thirty minutes the food finally came. My sliders were sliders—OK. But my wife didn't like her Brussel sprouts—too hard. And there was something wrong with her salmon which I no longer remember. She sent her whole dish back. Not unusual for her. And I picked at my sliders not to finish them too soon and have to sit there watching her eat ad infinitum.

Her salmon came back and I think it was OK. I don't really remember. She might have sent it back again. I had my short term memory knocked out of me when I was a pro boxer.

I can be glamorous. Look at me like those beautiful doors in Florence by whatever artist was thrilled with his own work. I am a marvel. A Ph.D. in poetry and a professional boxer. If only the diversity conscious left wing could find diversity in following my life style. I am manic. There's the pleasure. The lithium takes the edge off it but it keeps me from fighting with my wife and I am hyper about her.

As usual I wasn't paying attention to much of what she said. She'd always questioned me, "Are you hearing? Are you paying attention to me?"

"No," I said. "Well," I said, "It's time to go."

"We've only been here an hour," she said.

"Two," I said.

"Look at your watch," she said.

Then the waiter came over with some free deserts. Delicious. I don't remember whether they were ice cream or whipped cream. It didn't matter. Nothing matters unless it hurts.

The bill hurt. It was a hundred and twenty five dollars. Plus a twenty dollar tip. I paid and finally saw the opportunity to get out of there. I stood up and handed my wife her coat.

We went downstairs to the bathrooms and there was no one in the Men's Room. I went into a private stall, sat on the seat so no one could see my wanger and pissed. I was proud of myself. For someone who was piss shy I was almost piss bold.

I washed my hands to show off that I was bathroom savvy. I went into the hallway to wait for my wife. She was fast for her. Just five minutes. Amazing. Everything was falling into place.

We went outside to get a cab. She wanted to go to Fifth Avenue. I told her that that goes downtown and will cost me extra money. We grabbed a cab on Madison Avenue and went up to 72nd Street where we live.

Home at last. I welcomed hopping into our marble foyer. We went to our separate computers and wrote. That's what I really wanted to do anyhow. What's the sense in going out? It costs money. You see a bunch of people who you don't really know. You waste time. Time wastes you.

The world is superficial. I like being inside with myself and my wife. That is my circumference. That is my globe. I spin around her. I am beautifully alone with her. I don't have much time. I may have twenty years left. I want to luxuriate in the memory of the first seventy-two. I am resurrecting my past. I am fishing for myself in the receding waters.

The evening was a beautiful compromise. I did what I wanted. I did what I didn't. The owner of the St. Regis, John Jacob Astor, died like a gentleman. I hope I have his courage. I hope I drown ahead of my wife on the Titanic.

Big Time Tennis

My father had been in the insurance business his whole life. Well, he actually became a broker after WWII. During the war he was a navigator in a bomber over Italy and Germany. Seventy per cent of his fellow aviators died. Not good odds.
War is without regrets and kills for the fun of it. I was lucky that my dad survived to knock my mother up when he came back. My brother was born while he was overseas. We were a typical post war suburban family. We lived on the Upper West Side until my parents saved up enough money to buy a split level house in East Meadow. We had two cars and one garage. Our mood was middle class optimistic and our lawns were horizontal. There were no hills in East Meadow, my first real house when I was seven. All the lots were flat. The area was spanking new and there were no trees. It was like our block was a baseball field.

One thing I hated about insurance was insurance. I wanted to be a poet or an actor. My mom was a small theatre actress. I envied her. She was beautiful. Not so much my dad. But he made up for his short stature with a warm, sweet personality. I was close to him. Because he was five foot six inches tall I didn't want to be any taller than that. I wanted to be him. No Oedipal implications implied.

But I left my artistic dreams to follow him into the business world after graduate school in literature. I can't complain. I made a lot of money. I like what money buys. I don't care much about piling it up. I couldn't stand on money. I had to stand on my own soul.

I'll skip over thirty- nine years to talk about when I played the USTA national thirty-five and over in West Palm Beach. That made my father proud. He was a tennis fanatic even though he wasn't very good. If I hadn't been a businessman and made a lot of money I couldn't have afforded the coaching that made me a good player. I couldn't have afforded Steve Turner a few days a week. He had played the US Open and Wimbledon. He taught me top spin.

My dad played tennis with his commander in the airforce. He used it as a stepping stone to easier duties. When I was a kid I didn't know that my dad wasn't good. But I enjoyed his enjoying playing with me and after I turned twenty-five and became skilled he didn't take another set from me.

Later on I used tennis to score brownie points. I played with the most powerful people in insurance, the Greenbergs of AIG. I played at their Bedford estate on grass courts.

Before discussing the nationals I want to point out one tournament that I played at North Shore Tennis Club in 1985. It was the New York State Championships. I was thirty-eight years old. I wasn't yet the club champ. I wasn't even that good. But I was always challenging myself and entering things that were a bit beyond me.

I eventually became the champ of North Shore in 1987 but the States were only in 1985 and I had not yet fully developed my one hand top spin backhand. I think I eventually developed that from Villas. I also hadn't yet developed my steady game where I kept hitting to my opponent until he got bored and went for misplaced winners.

At this period of my life I was racking up a small fortune in the insurance business. Like all 80's youth I was doing some cocaine. I brought a small plastic bag with me to the New York States. Cocaine gave me confidence and I felt that it might help me playing in a big muck-a-muck tournament like the New York States.

About ten minutes before I was called out to play in the States I went into the men's room and did a couple of lines. When I came out I realized that the weather was in the nineties and that the coke might kill me. I didn't care. I wanted to win.

An official introduced me to my opponent. Let's call him Smith because due to brain injuries from a later-on pro boxing career I have trouble remembering anything.

Smith happened to be ranked number five in the state. I think. Well, he was ranked something.

In the warm up I saw that he had pretty good strokes. I didn't care. I was cocaine happy and an imitation of a champion. I was manic and self-congratulatory.

I set off running full tilt. Somehow I won the first three games. This was ridiculous. I wasn't nearly on his level. The cocaine raised my skill five hundred per cent.

People started gathering around our court to see the upset. Between games I realized that most of the coke had sweated out of my system. I was feeling shaky. My confidence was gone. I was a deflated balloon of fake ego. I could try to aggrandize my failure and blame it on the coke but it was the coke that gave me the first three games. Suddenly, I stank. I felt like a bus stop bathroom on the center of the court. After the initial games I didn't win another game.

When I finished the match there was no crowd around our court. I was no longer the upset attraction. I was a disappointment. I was a basketball that dribbled onto a size sixteen sneaker. I was a tennis ball that was hit over the fence.

What's the difference? I felt good that I had played in the States. I was on another level even though I was smashed. I was now David, the big tournament player. I was macho man.
****

I flew down to West Palm Beach by myself in 1988. This was my shot at the big leagues. I was signed up for the Nationals. I had five wooden Dunlap racquets under my arm and I looked like a pro. I was in first class. I was seated next to someone who everybody admired—Mickey Mantle.

People kept coming up to him asking for his autograph. He got a little drunk. He was a nice guy but I never respected baseball. I thought it was for non-athletic, chubby, middle-aged men. Of course, I didn't say anything to Mickey. I was discrete, polite and respectful even if I didn't respect his sport. I thought baseball players were chubby, non-athletes who trotted around the bases. I hated baseball. I hated all team sports.

I checked into a mediocre hotel near the tennis club. I was a small league guy who was playing in the big leagues.

The next day I showed up at the club and they gave me a polo shirt with the name of the tournament stitched into it.

The Nationals? Wow. I had made it. Actually, I had qualified for it because I was ranked No. 30 in New York State. No matter how badly I did in the States, I got a pass into the tournament.

I looked at the draw. I got el-stucko. I had to play a guy name Kramer who had just lost to Eddie Dibbs in the third round of the U.S. Open. I was excited and disappointed. I was proud to play such a high level appointment but I figured I'd get killed.

If I had to lose I might as well lose to a classy opponent with an international ranking.

I didn't realize that Kramer had the hardest serve in the tournament. I never liked serves. I was a ground stroker like Borg or Villas. I thought serve and volleyers were spoiled brats like McEnroe. They didn't want to do the hard work to stroke endlessly to win a point.

On the prime court a guy I knew from the Eastern Circuit, Ron Rueben, had just lost to a great player whose name I naturally forgot. Ron laughed to his friend when he was coming off the court and said, "I didn't even reach deuce."

I hoped that that wasn't a prognostication for me. But the first game I didn't even return one serve. Kramer didn't hit top spin but he sliced balls that skidded across the hard-tru. I hated slices. I thought they were effeminate. Real men hit topspin.

I was knocking my sneakers with my racquet trying to pick the sliders up. The guy was just too good for me. It was like I was lifting up buried balls. I mean I could beat almost any suburban player but this was another league. Kramer was the real thing and I was a near-do-well. At this level.

In the second set I managed to reach deuce. I was excited. Rueben never got so far and he was a tennis instructor in Great Neck. I felt I wasn't so bad. Only compared to the real pros.

The whole match lasted less than an hour. I giggled as I got off the court. I was a joke. I shook Kramer's hand like I was worthy of the gesture. Well, I was a small dot in the big leagues. I did my best. I didn't know anyone else either in business or back in my college days who could have done as well as I did even though I did badly.

I called my wife and we laughed on the phone. I felt like a kid who had lost his toys. I wasn't embarrassed. I was proud.

I mean what other insurance broker could have played at a national level and been embarrassed but not ashamed. I did it even if I didn't. I was a national player. I was someone. I was me regardless of other opinions of who I was.

I tried. And the effort of trying was the accomplishment. I kissed my hand. I was glad to know me.

Win or lose, I loved myself for trying.

Later I was told that the next day I would play a consolation round. This was for all te first round losers.

Maybe I would do well in this. That morning I was teamed up against a guy I knew from the Eastern Tennis Association. I think he name was Harrison. What do I know?

I was shocked when I lost to him badly. I'm not sure what the score was but it was something like 6-2, 6-1.

The guy wasn't on Kramer's level. I mean he could win your average club championship but he was no way on an international level. I felt a little worse about this loss than about my love-love loss to Kramer.

When I got back on the plane with my six racquets under my arm I felt like a champ. I told the guy sitting next to me and the stewardess that I just played the nationals. I felt like something else. What that was would later be determined as I competed in tennis, skiing and boxing. I was always there ready to compete. I was a good loser. And sometimes I won against tough competition and I was glad that I was me and had the courage to win or lose. It didn't matter. I just wanted to play the game.

Cheeky

I went over to Stan's house in Saddle Rock, a medium rich section of Great Neck. It wasn't as luxurious as King's Point but it wasn't a servants' area Spinny Hill either. His dad owned a chain of appliance stores. His stores were like Crazy Eddy's before that chain existed. I don't remember the name. I don't remember much after years of boxing, after years of not bothering to protect my head. Well, so be it. My future is more resonant than my past. Coincidentally I would share a dorm in prison years later with Eddie Antar's brother. His family actually owned Crazy Eddy's.

Stan's family sold discount appliances. His house was commodious but not glorious. It was somewhere between Nick Carraway's cottage and Gatsby's mansion. It was rich but not splendid.

I wasn't that friendly with Stan. He went to Great Neck South High and I went to North. He was a little too preppy for my taste. You know, the kind that wore the penny loafers and the Indian madras shirts. He was happy to be part of Great Neck's sculpted oppulence. He had no desire to cut his own swathe between the nouveau riche crowd, the manicured lawns and the fabulous houses. He was indicative of the rich suburbs. He was a neat landscape.

His family wasn't one of the super-rich. His father was probably worth a couple of million dollars a year. He didn't live with the multi-millionaires in a mansion on Kings Point. He could afford almost anything but did not have millions in the bank. He didn't own a yacht. His family had a four cars. They rented a private plane.

I rang the bell and Stan let me in. He was swarthy and about five foot seven. He took me down to the basement where Steve, Jimmy and Marc were playing pool.

I didn't know any of these kids too well because my family had just moved into Great Neck a couple of months ago. I was kind of flattered that Stan had invited me over. I was apidly becoming an insider. Still I felt a little out of joint.

Steve invited me to play pool. I was feeling a little out of it so I turned him down and went into the corner to watch some television. I don't know what I was watching because I was drifting on a canoe in my own world. I was happy to have a few friends but didn't know if this group was right for me. I turned over into the air bubble of my own self-consciousness.

Butch looked down at my black suede shoes and said, "You wearing shit kickers?"

"I like them," I said. I was feeling uncomfortable and sad. I felt like I had risen from earth and landed on another planet. I missed East Meadow where I felt comfortable among the middle class kids. I was here but I wasn't here. I was lonely. I felt like a broken statue in a museum.

"You would like those ugly shoes," Marc said. "You are going to have a tough time fitting into Great Neck if you dress like a rocka. The Great Neckians dressed preppy, like English mods.

"I do what I do," I said.
"Do, do," Steve said and laughed.
"Where's the bathroom?" I asked.
Stan pointed me to it.

When I closed the bathroom door I reached into my pocket and took out a switchblade. I don't know why I carried it. I never stabbed anyone. I wasn't tough. I was disturbed. I didn't even know how to knife fight.

But I was hurting from my faux friends' rejection. I felt I needed to cut myself. I took the sharp tip of the knife and pulled it down against my cheek. I didn't do it too hard. I was chicken. But I managed to eek out a thin line of blood.

I then did it on my other cheek and on my forehead. I washed the blood off as best I could and dried it with a bathroom towel. I then hid the bloody towel beneath the sink.

I felt proud. I had courage. I wondered if my friends would be scared of me when I came out of the bathroom. Would they think I was nuts? Was I nuts? No, I didn't kill myself. I wasn't really trying to hurt myself. I only made a little scratch.

I stepped outside the bathroom into the basement. Stan asked, "What did you do to your face?"

"Cut it up," I said.

"Why?" Stan asked. "We're going to have to sneak you out through the basement window so that my mother doesn't see you."

When I was outside I felt a breeze brushing against my cheek. It felt cool against my hot blood. I stopped under a tree and picked up some muddy leaves, wiping the cuts.

My house was about a mile from Stan's. I skipped along joyously. I was the blood man. I was the milk man. I was the walrus. I was Paul, the Beatles. This description was yet to come. The Beatles had not yet written "I am the Walrus."

When I got home I sneaked in through the garage and went up the back staircase to my room. I was quiet because I didn't want my parents to hear me.

In my room I looked for some crayons. I used black and brown ones to further smudge the mud I had on the cuts on my cheeks. I figured that I could pretend that I was beaten up by some kids and that they scraped my face on the ground.

I didn't want them to know that I had been cutting myself up with a knife. They might have worried about me. I didn't want to hurt them. I didn't want them to think that I was insane.

I wasn't insane. I had just had some compulsion to feel sorry for myself. I was sorry for myself. I felt out of joint in the rich town of Great Neck. I felt that I was disconnected from my body and a long distance from my soul.

It was ironic that my parents had moved to Great Neck to get me away from the bad environment in East Meadow. Yet I had never sliced myself up in the Meadow. The luxury of Great Neck had somehow made me feel out of sorts. I wanted to hurt myself. I didn't feel that I was as pretty as the houses. I was in the servant's quarters of resentment. I couldn't get along with myself or my friends. I was an outcast.

It occurred to me that I had become self-destructive since I moved to Great Neck. Yet my parents had moved me there to get me into a better school distruct and to help me to be a better student.

I was just playing with the self-destruction. I wanted to see who I was and how far I would go. I didn't think that there was a chance that I would kill myself. But who knows? I was just cutting the surface.

A REAL PISSER

I dumped my wife in the Astor Court at the St. Regis Hotel after our tea sandwiches. Well, I didn't exactly dump her but I couldn't stick around because I had to piss. I did not like to piss in public. I went downstairs to the men's room. I passed the urinals. No way I would stand in front of one of them and put my wanger out in the air. That would be disgusting.

I went into one of the two stalls. When I pulled my penis out I felt that I was flashing the walls. I was not worried that someone else would come into my stall but that they would enter the general bathroom and that I would know that they were there and would get the creeps.

I sat on the toilet seat to try to get some cover from possible intruders. It didn't help. I think I smelled a stench from the neighboring stall. Sometimes I imagine bad things. I got up and walked to the sink and swallowed some water. I went back in the stall and spit it on my groin. This usually worked but it didn't.

Maybe I had mistimed it. Perhaps I had last pissed only two hours ago instead of three. The chronology of bladder relief is a precise science. Maybe I wasn't ready yet to rain into the bowl.

I went back upstairs to the dining room and told my wife I had to go home—seventeen blocks—to piss. She was none to happy. She pointed out to me the times I deserted her at society parties and charity events because I didn't feel the conditions were conducive to piss.

I told her I'd go home, piss, and then come back. Not much of a consolation when our apartment was seventeen blocks away. But I am what I am—I am David the neurotic-about-piss man. They call it being piss shy. I call it, "the slobs of the world conspire against me." I don't like elimination. Water backs up in me like emotions I can't let loose.

As for a dump? You can forget that possibility. I don't do that in public. I'd rather burst.

I walked over to Madison Avenue and grabbed a bus. Before it took off an elderly homeless type of man started yelling at the driver, holding us up. Being an ex pro boxer I thought of beating his face in. He was a nuisance who deserved to be quieted. When he was down I would have kicked him in the balls like I used to do to friends as a teenager. I don't pity people who are in my face. I want to bite off their noses. I'm afraid of piss but not of violence.

Somehow the confrontation didn't happen and I rode the bus to Seventy-Second Street. When I got upstairs I pissed with the greatest of ease like a coward mastering the trapeze. I was so relaxed I almost felt like jerking off.

It was so easy. So natural. Like the childhood saying that everything was satisfactual.

I called my wife bragging, "I pissed." Then I asked if she wanted me to come back now.

She said she'd call back later. I wondered if she was flirting. Maybe my piss-histrionics made her want to leave me. Maybe she couldn't just understand that I was weird and had certain inhibitions.

She was married to a nut. She shouldn't try to crack me. She should soften me up so that I fit into her bra. She should make me her own not a trombone that slides into her equanimity. She should love me for my differences not for the way I fit in with the general trend of humanity. Sameness is boring. I was different.

I called back later. She said she was now at Amarinth eating blueberries and that if I didn't pay for her blueberries I wasn't welcome.

"I already paid a hundred dollars towards your taxes at H&R Block earlier, eighty dollars for lunch and sixteen dollars for the cab. I don't plan on paying for blueberries," I said.

"Then you're not welcome here," she said.

"You're welcome," I said and hung up.

This getting used to being poor was not easy. I once was rich and chauffeured around in a Rolls Royce. Not that I really cared. But she did. What was I to do? I was seventy-two and had no real earning potential. I could never return her old lifestyle to her.

I was a real pisser. But I couldn't even piss in a public place. I was removing myself from the earth. I wanted to run. I wanted to hide. I wanted to come up on the earth's other side with no one around to watch me be what I be.

And that is me. Hard to get along with but lovable despite my foibles. Just ask my wife. No, better not. I don't mean to be irritating. Irritating just happens to be me. I don't like me that much. But I am attracted to me.

A Bit of Insane

Maybe I am insane. Maybe I am not. I hope I am. I want to have something exciting like *dementia pugilistica.* There is something romantic about brain injuries. You don't know whether you are coming or going and you struggle for direction. You can't navigate with broken wings. Your oars have holes in them.
And you don't need excuses for your behavior or your comments because you are your behavior and can't escape your condition.

I do have tremors but it could be from the lithium. My psychopharmacologist calls it *tardive disconesia.* I am unsteady on my feet and muscularly slow. I sometimes get confused and lose my direction or my thoughts.
I trip on my face. I forget who I am and your name and yours and yours. I get confused when I climb down the stairs in the subway. I don't know which foot to put in front of the other one. I want to stand on my head and bounce down the stairs like a ball. I sometimes trip. I get confused between left and right.

I ask my neurologist if I have Parkinson's. He says that he doesn't think so. I am not Mohamed Ali nor was I meant to be. I wrote a book by the name *Dementia Pugilistica.* It's poems. Poems are vague and catch waves in cups. My definition of meaning is bewilderment. I can't tell this from that or the meaning of absence. I don't know what I am saying. But I do. And I am writing these ideas as a story because no one wants to make the effort to understand poems.

It could have been drugs not boxing that caused my *dementia.* But it wasn't. I used to like being punched like I enjoyed snorting cocaine. It was the same feeling as an orgasm when I came. A brilliant numbness. Glue was like that. A kind of elastic tingle.

When I get hit my brain cells die and the past falls into cellophane, prophylactic coffins. I become what was and the present is buried in the box of the past.

I'm sorry but I like getting punched. It makes me fall in love with my own injuries and sorrow. It reminds me of the occasional punishments I got from my parents when I was a boy. The pitty pat slaps in the face from my mother.

Sometimes when I get hit my past falls into cellophane coffins where my death is translucent. In my insanity I am riding light at the comet rodeo. Or am I a wet suit at a mirage? Or am I a seal clapping rubber fins?

I am lost in a body bag of madness and I wear Arabic name tags that rebel against me. There is no honor in honor killings. I am Islamophobic. I am proud of it. I don't cherish enemies. I am angry. I believe in revenge. Saith me, not the Lord.

The cops draw chalk outlines around my mind. Yesterday vanishes like jay walkers. I am the accident that never happened.

You think that I am jealous of your sanity. Not a drop. I am lost in the leisure of not caring.

****

I am frenetic but you want me to slow down, to park in your ethics. I value your values but I don't always agree with them. I am not pedestrian. I am a winged horse.

You ticket me with your opinions. I pay the fine. And twenty years later I remember the heavy bag in prison and the way the thugs respected me because they had seen me knock someone out on national television. A mafia guy name Stevie saw me fight an exhibition with Macho Comacho at the Taj Mahal in Atlantic City.

In jail I bobbed and weaved under wicked angels. I was as light as a disappearing crime. I beat on the heavy bag and coached the criminal animals to pick thorns from their knuckles.

I wished I hadn't evaded my taxes. It's such a nerdy crime. I wanted to beat someone to death and become a long-term convict. I wanted to be tough, not a crooked book keeper. *Men's Journal* once wrote an article about me--*America's Oldest Pro Wants to Kill Someone.*

I worked out with Pauli Moore from the Whitey Bulger gang. When you are in jail you respect gangsters. He used to spar with Marvin Hagler. He told me he was offered a football scholarship to college but felt it was cooler to become a gangster. I liked Pauli but he had low life values. I never imagined someone would want to be a gangster. Where I come from we wanted to be brain surgeons.

The jail doctor put me on lithium. He didn't like my rhythm on the speed bag. He thought I was out of step with reality. He wanted to straighten me out. He thought there was hope against hope and nothing to achieve no matter what.

My wife had called him and told him that I was manic depressive. I disagreed but in the long run I think she was right.

****

When I got out of jail I returned to Gleasons Gym every day. I pretended to my parole officer that I had a job there and he let me attend. Boxing makes me smile. I fight against failure and taxes and the water ballet of the dead. I keep my hands down so I can absorb punches to the face.

My friend told me that he was on early disability because he told social security that he was insane. I didn't think I could do that but I tried.

When I was interviewed at the social security office I was shocked that they certified me as insane. I thought that I was totally sane and a genius. I got early disability. I learned to think like a failure. I enjoyed being an ex con. I walked on soda bubbles. I was given a pension for the same mania that landed me in jail.
I actually started getting social security twenty years ago. Plus they gave me twenty-thousand dollars for back pay.

I remember when I took my physical for Vietnam and I failed for mental reasons. I am proud of seeming insane. I don't know why. I guess it makes me different in a special way. It is also useful and profitable. Insanity got me out of the draft and give me early social security. Being insane was a kind of a job.

****

I never applied for a real job again after my stint at Schuylkill Federal Prison Camp. I enjoyed picking up spare change from teaching boxing. When I was in insurance I was one of the top people in the industry. I didn't want to go back and be a lowly clerk. I was too proud to be a flunky. There was something classier about being an almost failure.

But I spent a few hours a day writing books. I wrote memoirs and poetry books. My published memoirs were *The King of White Collar Boxing* and *On Jail: The Essays.* Two of my poetry books were *Lane Changes* and *Living on Madison Avenue.* I also rewrote a novel which I started in jail—*In the Suburb of Possible Suicide.* That was published in 2020 by Adelaide Publishers. I received a contract from Eyewear Publishing in the U.K. for *Broken Paragraphs* .

I published hundreds of articles in *Daily Caller, Canadian Forum* and *American Thinker.* American and foreign magazines were always writing articles about me. I was the businessman who went into boxing to go from riches to rags. I was the Wall Street Rapper. I was the Rolls Royce fighter.

It seems that when I was writing books I could think straight. I was confused during the day but clear-headed when I was writing. I wanted to duck away from the world and find myself in my poems. I was part of the language. I was English. I believed in American. I didn't want to learn any other languages. Why should I speak broken French or German or Spanish when I was eloquent and beautiful in English? I'd rather speak one language well than five languages badly. I am not superficial. I am as deep as hidden, natural grammer.

Seeing My Recent Shrink

I am walking from Union Square subway station over to the mental clinic (Bernstein Pavilion) at Mt. Sinai/Beth Israel. It's not that I belong in such a grungy, freebee place. I'm used to private, overcharging shrinks. I'm a kind of classy guy who was bred like a show dog by upper middle class parents. Not that I'm a snob or a slob. I'm me—a bipolar constellation in the great sky, a wonderful guy, a resort in the rich Caribbean.

I am the Rolls Royce I used to be chauffeured in when I was a millionaire. Before I ditched my life style by getting caught in some trivial tax evasion. A minor league crime. I didn't even kill anyone. There's no glamor unless you use a hammer. Not that I mean that. But I do. I hate to go down for white collar details. I am not a mousey clerk. I don't belong in the subways with the shouting unwashed. I am not one of the poor who obsesses about money.

How did I get from my rich pscyhopharmacologist to this treatment for the poorly insane at the Bernstein Pavillion? In the waiting room, I was surrounded by chinos and shapeless dresses. Well, Jesse, my uptown shrink knew that I was short on funds and recommended me to the clinic. Nice of him, I have to admit.
He saved me from the loneliness of insanity. I was surrounded by other mental misfits. I was in the welfare clinic of the maladjusted. I didn't mind. Jessse told me that I might be put off by the look of the other patients. He forgot that I had been in jail and was used to ugliness.

And my new shrink, the chief resident, Michael Rosenthal, was a sweetheart who gave me forty minutes for $14 to ramble on about my favorite subject—myself. Jesse only gave me ten minutes for $275. Jesse prescribed medicine. That's why he was able to charge so much. After a year with Michael he was also able to give me medicines too. But his rates didn't go up. I owed Michael to Jesse.

I was in a clinic with broken birds who could only fly with one wing. The world felt sorry for me. I smiled. I celebrated my sad situation. I was a happy failure.

I passed a little girl on Third Avenue. I thought of raping her. These thoughts were what Michael called intrusive. They didn't mean anything. They were just distractions to make me hate myself.

I was thinking that I would run out of money and my wife would leave me. Twenty five years ago when I went bust and to jail I squirreled away a little money. At forty-nine I supplemented that with early disability social security. My wife earned some money from writing books and writing a Dream column for the *Daily News.* We survived. Barely. But we still held on to our three bedroom apartment on Madison Avenue. We were squatters in our own former luxury. We were the poorest people in our coop.

I thought of throwing myself in front of a subway car. I was capable of meeting destruction head on. I had been knocked out in my professional fight career in Denver and Boston. Don't forget when I was knocked cold as an amateur at Gleason's arena. I got a concussion, separated my shoulder and tore ligaments. But I wasn't afraid. Well, a little. I didn't want to get mangled. I wanted to be a pretty corpse like James Dean or Sal Mineo. It was actually John Derek as Pretty Boy Romano in the movie "Knock on any Door" who said, "I wanna live fast, die young, and leave a beautiful corpse." I liked the attitude. When I went to jail I was happy. I liked to make the best out of the worst. If your condition depressed you the outside world won. I wanted to be a winner while I was a loser.

I had been in therapy most of my life. At seventeen I threatened to commit suicide and my mom sent me to a psychiatrist-*cum*-cook in Great Neck. He was fat. He ate up my confusion and turned me into a productive human being. I did a five year stint with Big Al. He turned me from a self-destructive little druggie into a sober straight A student.

Twenty years later I went to Janet Wolf at Rational Behavior Institute. I lasted a few years but was not thrilled by her formulaic techniques. She was part of the Alfred Adler School of therapy.

In jail I saw the shrink who told me I was manic depressive. I didn't believe him at first. He didn't believe me that I fought pro, did rap albums, was a published poet and a millionaire who had a Ph.D. I also did a movie and modelled. It wasn't my fault I was so grand. I really was. He seemed not to believe me. I was superman with ambidextrous talents. I didn't belong with the other convicts who could hardly read. I still liked them. I flow. I am a river of personalities.

Out of jail I went to a few social workers—not memorable. One was gay. How could he understand me? I had quite a track record with women. I didn't want to be homophobic but I dropped him to protect my own safety net. I wanted to fall into something familiar, not a gay world I couldn't identify with. I was not homophobic. I was holistically phobic.

I went into the Bernstein Pavilion at Perlman Place. I had to show three forms of identity to get past the door. It wasn't like this last year. They must have had an incident on a day I wasn't there. It must have been some self-righteous nut who cracked at the wrong moment and left shells for others to pick up.

I checked in on the second floor and waited about a half an hour. I was always early. I don't know why. I guess I was afraid that being late would leave a bad impression, would connote rudeness, would be turning my back on my own cure.

Finally, Dr. Mike came out exactly on time. I always looked forward to seeing him. He was about half of my age. I was seventy-two. Dying, dead, resurrecting, who knows?

I was glad that he could give me forty minutes unlike my psychopharmacologist who only gave me ten. Not that I didn't like Jesse. I was with him fifteen years. It's just that I could only afford to see him once ever ten weeks in drips and drabs. And I liked to talk on and on. Particularly about myself.

But today was not a crazy day. It had nothing to do with my contrarian thoughts and my fragmented logic. I was not going to discuss my senile memory and the brain damage I had received in boxing. I was not even going to venture into my manic depression. Gotta tell you something. Six months ago Dr. Mike called in the world's expert on bipolars and displayed me for all the other young doctors. The residents asked me questions. I felt like the star of the mentally ill world. At the end of the session the King of Bipolarity said, "You are definitely bipolar." I never fully believed that even when the shrink in jail said it. I was too great to be bipolar. I was a genius. I was not some sick toad hopping around a diseased garden.

But I felt good. I liked being labelled. It defined me. Like Robert Frost I liked fences. Borders allow nationalities and divide the mind into fruitful dialectic. Separation allows real closeness.

Back to now. My snotty coop board decided that I should replace my windows because a window dropped a mile away. Of course that had nothing to do with our building. But snobs will be snobs and most of my neighbors who still had good jobs didn't give a damn. Also I had the most windows to replace and they might have liked sticking it to me because I was a boxer rather than a divorcee or an accountant. The windows could cost me fifty thousand dollars. I didn't have the money.

Michael said, "Don't get ahead of yourself. Check with an engineer. See if there is really a threat. Are you feeling suicidal?"

"A little. But I wouldn't look good with steel in my face. I am the third rail, the difference, the oddity, the genius. I do not belong dead on the tracks."

"So go with the flow."

"I'm flowing. I am a tributary. I am a bird. I glow. I know what I know and don't know what I don't know."

"You seem poetic today. Have you taken your lithium?"

"Now you sound like my wife. She can always tell when I am manic."

"Are you?

“No. But I don’t like the dimwits of the coop board putting out my lights. I should shine. Ugliness around me. Midgets wanting to be tall.”

Michael told me he’d be out for two weeks because he was going to London with his fiancé to pick a place to get married. He said, “You influenced me when you said you wanted to hold your wife’s hand and walked off the cliff to death. I saw eternity in my own relationship. That’s not common these days.”

“You see,” I said, “You can even learn things from madmen. I would charge you what you charge me but your rates are too low. Now if I could just charge you Jesse’s rates.”

We stood up and shook hands. He was more like a friend than a psychiatrist. It is true that he was half my age but what he gave up in authority he gave back in comradery.

I felt a little bad. “Fifty years ago I wanted to become a psychiatrist. But my psychiatrist back then told me, ‘You’re not really interested in other people. You are just interested in yourself.’”

Because of him I switched my major to literature straight through to my Ph.D. Lot of good it did me now. And he wasn’t really right. All he was interested in was cooking and I wanted to talk about my problems and talk to other people about theirs.

After my session I walked to the 6 train to go back to Gleason’s Gym. I couldn’t help but feel happy and sad. I liked my life style and loved my wife. But I was worried that the cost of the windows could take it all away from me. For all I knew it could be fifty thousand dollars. It’s ironic that when I was rich twenty-five years ago I offered to put in all new windows and the board said the landmark commission wouldn’t let me. Now when I was broke they insisted on their stupid windows.

The coop board even made up the lie that wooden windows were not ecologically sound. It’s just the opposite. The board didn’t know what they were doing but they carried their righteous banner like an army of invaders into the innocent tenants’ lives. What real man would sit on a coop board? Only a clerk or a thief.

The snotty board should take some Mucinex. In the eighties I was more successful than any of them. But I never tried to hurt anyone. I looked for the common good. Even though I was a professional boxer.

When I got to York Street on the subway I went to Forager's and got some prepackaged sushi. It was delicious. For twelve dollars they put out better sushi than Nobu who charged hundreds. I liked bargains. My life had become a bargain.

I went into my private office in Gleason's, ate my sushi, and took a nap. I was home. I had two homes—Gleason's in Brooklyn and Madison Ave in Manhattan with my wife. I never wanted to be anywhere else. I was what I be-ed when I be-ed in my two domiciles. Buy me a first class plane ticket around the world and I wouldn't go. I was not looking to explore the outer world but enter more deeply into myself.

I am seventy-two. I am Fred Astaire and Ginger Rogers dancing in my own movie. I don't want to step off the stage. I don't want to be part of the audience. I want to be continuously interviewed by the world's leading expert on manic depression. I was a star.

My student showed up—Patrick. He was a creative director for an advertising firm. He was thirty-three years old. He had been with me about five years and he was good.

I asked him, "Do you want to spar"

"I don't want to hurt an old man," he said.

We had sparred hundreds of times. The joking insult would have hurt me but the coop board had weakened me with their window-nonsense.

So we did drills. And even though I had the possiblre cost of the new windows hanging over my head my day was happy. I was living for myself, not for some distant job in the insurance industry. I was pleasantly broke. I had found the better way by losing my way.

I chuckled to myself when I fantasized that one day I would hire my old Rolls Royce chauffer and have him walk in front of me in his cap on the subway. Now that would be funny. I would impress my lower class peers. I had made it good. I would pretend that I was rich. A chauffeur in the subway. Now that was classy and different. Would my student or my psychiatrist want a lift?

Eye Fear

This morning on my way to the subway to go to Gleason's Gym I felt retrospectively trembly when I thought about how I used to be afraid that I would pick up a pencil and shove it into my eye.

Gooey.

Echh.

Oh the dark is dark and I wanted to poke the light out of its jar. I wanted to smash my cornea. Rip my retina.

This poking eye fear began around the time I went to Schuylkill Federal Prison camp in 1993. I was there for tax evasion. A nothing crime. I was not violent despite my fantasies. I was a lamb who imagined himself a wolf.

When I sat at a tiny desk in my dorm that I shared with my celli I would become fearful that my hand would take the pencil I was writing screenplays with and blind myself. I don't know why. It was instinctual, genetic, suicidal. Poking my eyes out was exactly what I didn't want to do so I pretended that I did want to do it to make myself suffer for everything I had done wrong in my life, my failure in business, my inability to be a better husband.

I would imagine my eye dripping in blobs like a Sunnyside-up egg. I would shake, tremble. Put the pencil down and sit on my hands till the self-destructive moon passed and I could return to my writing. When I was no longer afraid of blinding myself, the words tumbled out like a bandit escaping from the cops. I remembered when the FBI fingerprinted me in Delaware and complemented me on my fight on Sean O'Grady's Thursday Night Fights. I got a kick out of that. I was thrilled by whom I was, wasn't and pretended I was.

Of course my productivity would not last too long after my hands returned to the desk and I would once again find myself sitting on my hands. I didn't want my hands to escape from my butt and poke my pupils. The thought of blinding myself was hideous.

Obviously, blindness would interfere with my creativity and it would take me longer than I should to write my film scripts.

I didn't write novels because there were too many words and my knuckles would begin to hurt from sitting on my fingers. But there's a lot of white space between lines and characters in a film script and the medium was conducive to avoiding blinding myself. I had spent half of my life in psychoanalysis and I wondered if I were in some way Oedipal or I was a reverse Narcissus afraid to look in the pond at the beautiful irresponsibility I had become.

I thought I might have been a victim of my father's pedophilia. Only my father was no pedophile. I imagined he had felt me up only to make myself a special kind of victim. But he never touched me. Except when he occasionally hit me.

Dad was no perv. He was never the reason that I wanted to blind myself or didn't want to blind myself or was just afraid that I would. I blamed my potential self-destruction on psychological clichés and Greek legends.

In exploring my eye poking it occurred to me that my current psychiatrist, Michael at Mt. Sinai hospital, told me that he thought blindness was an intrusive thought like my thoughts when I walked down the street that I would rape a ten-year-old girl.

Never have I touched a woman or a girl inopportunely. I am the gentleman of gentleman. But ugly thoughts from outer space intrude. Why? Because I want to digress from practical problems that I might be able to wrestle with. I don't want solutions. I want to hurt myself.

I want to lose myself in unreal fantasies of self-destruction so that I am lost in the yellow brick road of cowardice where pragmatism is an awkward situation.

I don't want answers. I want to suffer. I want to get lost in another planet and find myself in orbit. I want to die while breathing. I want confusion to settle on me like a warm blanket so that I don't know who I am and don't really care.

I am on the subway going home from the gym. I think a terrorist is going to pull a gun from his knapsack and shoot me. I know that it's just a fantasy but I get out at the next stop and wait for another train.

I am almost hoping that I hear gun shots or an explosion coming from the train I just escaped. I am saving myself for the non-existent afterlife. I will be dramatic and beautiful. I do not know if I will be able to see myself.

I think back to when I was a lovely, sweet child. All the relatives said that I had goo goo eyes and the longest lashes.

How did I become a con who was obsessed with killing himself? But I didn't really want to commit suicide. I wanted to feel the sweet tenderness of injuries like dancing cheek to cheek with sadness.

With a Stone

I am not violent. I was gently violent when I was seventeen. I don't know why. I liked to beat my friends up but not to kill them. Maybe I was afraid of them and wanted to knock them unconscious so they wouldn't kill me. You can call me David. I know you can't call me. But I am the fear that catches in the throat of my own self. I am failure. Or I was.

The thought of losing a fight to my pals was horrendous. I didn't want to be embarrassed. I tried to knock them out so that they wouldn't kill me. My punches were prophylactic. My opponents didn't get pregnant with destruction or fat with death.

So many fights. Which one to describe? Like it wasn't obvious that my bloodiest, killer-like fight would be against Butch Orbach. I still feel guilty about that one to this day. Well, maybe not guilty. Maybe just queasy. Afterall, he was a close friend. He was crazy but when I was with him I felt like I had entered into the warm evil of the universe.

But let's hold up on that fight. I actually fought an earlier fight that day. It seems I fought a double header.

That was the year that I was graduating from my junior year in Great Neck North High School. It was smack-in-your-face summer when I went with my friends to Flushing Meadow's World Fair.

I was at the World's Fair with Butch and a few other kids. I'm not sure who they all were and how many of them hung with us. I never paid attention to details. To me they were petty. I didn't care. About anything and about the nothing that absconded from the game.

I guess two of the kids at the Fair were Lex and Steve. For sure, Mad Dog. I am seventy-two now and having had a pro fight career I have acquired a bit of dementia. Memory is not one of my strong points. I don't even respect the past. I am fascinated with my limited future. I want to create. I want to tell this story.
Even if I have to reinvent it.
My group of delinquent friends were the worst lot from Great Neck. They acted more like the tuffs in Uniondale and Levittown. We aspired to be low class even though we were rich. We wanted to be tough. It was the middle sixties and peace and love a la the Beatles had not yet quite come in. We were still putting hair cream in our hair. We wore Old Spice aftershave. Buddhism and love were still stuck in the suburbs of California. Here, greasers still took predominance over hippies.

Lex was a Christian kid who was even a little lower than low class. He was a hanger on. He looked like his next bath would be his first. He was not really my friend, not one of my in crowd. His teeth were stained from smoking. He rolled his own tobacco and there were flakes on his shirt. His fingernails were black. He was a slob. His sharp cheek bones looked like he was already pointing at the knife of his own death. He stank. At life and at everything including his underarms. He failed at failing even though he failed.

For some reason Lex started a fight with me. Fights were their own reason. There cause was superfluous. They happened like a morning sunrise. They were their own weather. And as Lex rained punches down on me I put on my resilient poncho of numbness and felt less than nothing. I didn't know that I was tough even though I was tough enough.

I threw Lex to the ground, straddled his head with my knees and kept punching him in the nose and lips. He was a bloody Mary. A delicious drink of failed humanity. He couldn't even beat me up and I was a spoiled brat. I was from the Jewish part of Great Neck, living in a quasi mansion. He should have been able to kill me. He was a Christian not a pussy Jew. But he couldn't even live up to his punkyness. He might as well have worn one of my people's yamulkas and felt guilty for anti-communism.

Like a true adolescent I let him up all bloody faced and I apologized for hurting him. It always startled me the way teenagers beat each other up and then let bygones be bygones and forgave each other. If I had killed him I would have probably wanted to be friends with his corpse.

"I'm sorry I started the fight ," Lex said, generously.

"Didn't mean to hurt you," I said.

"Never apologize for blood and bruises," my friend Mad Dog said.

"You want to fight?" Lex said to Mad Dog. Not that Mad Dog would have. He was all snarl and no bite. He was scared of his own shadow, his dark bark.

Stevie didn't say anything. He was not a fighter. He was good at physics.

Butch said, "I'll fight you Mad Dog."

We all moved behind the Belgian Waffle House to watch the fight between Mad Dog and Butch. I was surprised that bluffer Mad Dog would actually fight. He was a congenital chicken. And Butch was a fairly tough guy who claimed he had been in a lot of street fights in Paris when he lived there with his divorced dad.
We found an empty alcove in the back of the exhibition buildings.

Mad Dog and Butch squared off. Mad Dog was shaking like a mobile exhibit in the World's Fair. Butch started pushing the Dog around. He slapped him with the back of his hand. He wasn't really trying to hurt him as much as trying to humiliate him.

Mad Dog turned his back to Butch in order to run away. Butch punched him in the back of the head.

That was enough for me. I didn't like Butch taking advantage of Mad Dog. I stepped in between them. I had to protect the little coward.

Butch pushed me.

"I don't want to fight," I said to Butch.

"Then you shouldn't have stepped in front of me," he said and spit in my face.
That pissed me off to no end. I didn't like dirty fighting. And spit was certainly dirty. I grabbed Butch in a headlock and threw him to the ground. I lost it and stuck my fingers in his mouth and started pulling his lips apart until they bled.
We rolled over on each other.

There were some big rocks around us. He grabbed my ear and pulled it. I picked up a rock and started pounding his head. Butch covered his skull with his hands. I think I broke his fingers which were now bleeding along with his head. It was a blood bath. None of our friends dared to step in to break it up.

Time moved slowly as I cracked his skull. I didn't want to kill him. So I pounded it at a medium pace. Little pieces of skin broke loose from his hair. I thought I was being nice by not hitting him harder with the rock.

Mad Dog yelled, "Cut it out or I'll beat you two up." Of course, Mad Dog never beat anyone up. He should have changed his name to puppy dog.

Butch was out cold. I felt safe. I wanted him to be unconscious so that he wasn't able to attack me again. I sat on top of him like a conquering warrior. I looked around me for no reason. Then I saw three cops running down the alley to where we were lying.

The cops grabbed me off Butch and put us both against the wall. Our friends sneaked away while the cops were tagging us.

Mad Dog turned around and yelled at the cops, "Bet you can't catch me" and took off full throttle.

A fat cop, looking like Oliver Hardy with a crew cut, asked, "What's going on here? Are you kids crazy? You want to be locked up?"

His co-star cop, Stan Laurel, looked at me and said, "You could have killed this kid."

And Harpo made hand signals of distress.

I said, "We're friends. We were just arguing over a girl. It's nothing."

Hardy said, "Nothing. Wait till your parents see you."

Butch said, "I don't have a mother."

Laurel said, "You're lucky we're in a generous mood. We're not going to take you to the station house. We're just going to kick you out of the Fair."

"Fair enough" Butch said.

People stared at us as we walked, a bloody sight, ahead of the cops out to the entrance to the World's Fair.

When they kicked us out of the turnstile the cops yelled, "And don't come back or you'll end up in jail."

As we left Butch turned around and gave the cops the finger. He was stupid like that. I was kind of glad that I beat him up. He deserved it.

My other friends were out of sight. I guess they didn't want to be smeared with our guilt. They probably had called their parents and told them to pick them up.

Butch and I got on the Long Island railroad to Great Neck. Butch went into the bathroom and got some toilet paper. He tried to damp down the blood on his head. He was a mess.

"You shouldn't have busted me up," Butch said.

"You shouldn't have messed with Mad Dog. You know he can't fight."

"Not your business," Butch said.

"Maybe," I said. "I have no business. I'm a kid."

"Me too," Butch said. And we made silly faces at each other and everything was all right again. At least it seemed to be. We were at that forgiving stage.

When we got out at Great Neck train station we walked about a mile to my French Provcial mansion in the Estates.

We were best buddies again. We were young men and didn't hold grudges. We forgave. We were forgiven.

We sneaked in a back door at my house and went up to my room. My parents were in their large room with the turrets and didn't hear us.

I slipped Butch into my mirrored bathroom and turned on the shower for him. I left the room and let him wash the blood out of his hair and off of his fingers. About twenty minutes later he came out of the bathroom all new and shiney. He started dancing around my bedroom like Mick Jagger. He had that look with the big lips and all.

"I'm sorry I almost killed you," I said.

"You would have done me a favor."
****

Ten years later I was on vacation in Barcelona and I ran into him. He was on a motorcycle and driving through the traffic like a maniac.

I was always worried that even though we had forgiven each other that he might one day seek revenge and kill me.

We chatted for about twenty minutes about our past. Then he took off, speeding on his bike. I guess that was for best. There was some dangerous chemistry between us. We might mix up our personality ingrediants badly. We might explode.

He drove his motorcycle like a maniac. I worried that he might kill himself. Maybe that would be for the best and get me out of his possible revenge.

Max's Kansas City

I was at Max's Kansas City with my friends Kenny and Bruce. We were caught in the middle of 1969. We were in the brain washed correctness of the hippy era. We took our irresponsibilities seriously. We were proud of being irrelevant and a hop skip and a jump from sensibility. We were opinionated. We were arrogantly right when we were wrong. We predated the political correctness of the Obama era. We were left wing. We hated Senator McCarthy.

That era would much later be celebrated in a song by the Eagles, "Hotel California." There was that famous line, "'We haven't had that spirit here since nineteen sixty nine." But we weren't an afterthought by the Eagles. We were plop squat in our 69 generation. In fact we were 1969. We were at 213 Park Avenue South at Max's Kansas City in that very famous year.

We were there two to three nights a week for five years. After that I never went back. It was as if my house burned down to forgetfulness. My past was cremated. The excitement of the era disappeared into the urn of days past.

Max's back room was filled with freaks from the Andy Warhol gang. Tie dye jeans and floral shirts. Long hair and dirty faces. One big blond was walking around topless.
A black drag queen was sashaying around between the tables. She stuck her fake tits into Bruce's face. He didn't know what to do so he just sat there and sucked it up. Not the tits. The embarrassment.

Ingrid Superstar came over to me and said, "Hi Donavan." She thought I looked like him. I did. She had a crush on the me that was not me, on Sunshine Superman.

Bruce, Ken and I were sitting down drinking wine and eating chick peas. We thought we were cool. Upstairs Lou Reed was reciting some of his songs. His voice was flat. He was talky. His fans didn't know the difference. For some reason he was cool to them. Years later I imitated him when I became a rapper.

We were happy with the Warhol crowd. They were like another planet that we were visiting.

Bruce handed out some pills to us.
"What are these" I asked.
"Mescaline," Bruce said.
"What's that?" I asked.
"I'll try them," Ken said.
We washed them down with wine. I shouldn't have. But I was into taking chances. Besides I didn't want to seem chicken. I had never done acid. I didn't realize there were some parallels with mescaline. I wouldn't have tried it if I had known that it was an hallucinogenic. I had a tendency towards psychosis that frightened me. I had done small stuff like pot, hash, dexatrine, glue and plastic wood.

The summer before I had done horse tranquilizers on Cape Cod and was so zonked that I was wearing a leather jacket in ninety-five degree weather. I sat down next to a picnicking family and told them that I loved them. I was part of the generation of peace and love. I was a cliché mouthing platitudes. I was chewing on a piece of peace pie.

*****

I remembered drugs before the hippy era. My grubby friend, Larry, had taken me to a heroin shooting gallery in Harlem. We were just copping pot but we saw four or five skanks shooting up heroin. One greaser's arm swelled up and turned blue.
We gave a toothless skinny guy ten dollars to go out and get us a dime bag of weed. He took the money gladly. We hung around

the heroin shooters uncomfortably. When the toothless guy who had gone out to cop our pot came back he said, "I was robbed." Sure. Like we weren't fish in a shark tank. Let it go. He robbed us. Who cared? At least we didn't shoot heroin.

We lost ten dollars but got out of there while the getting was good. I swore to myself that I would never do heroin. It was gross. Twenty years later I saw the movie—"Trainspotting." Heroin made the hero shit in his pants. I was bathroom phobic. I'd never shoot heroin.

*****

I didn't feel much after the mescaline for about a half an hour. Ingrid Superstar came back over to me and winked at me. Her eye looked huge and amorous. I was scared of her. She looked like an octopus who might swallow me up.

It occurred to me that reality was becoming unreal. There was a tilt to everything. Like our lives might fall on the floor. Like we might have to vacuum up reality. Like I was in a cave with creatures from other planets. Like a precursor of Star Wars.

I was beginning to feel different like I was floating a little outside myself and looking back in through my eyes. "Let's go for a walk." I told Ken. Bruce said, "I'll stay here, at Max's."

Ken and I started walking down town. His parents had rented him an apartment a few blocks away. We headed in that direction.

I was beginning to become confused. Fifty years later I sometimes feel disoriented like that. My neurologist says that it is a form of dementia from being hit in the head so much when I was a boxer. But when I was twenty-one I hadn't boxed yet. A few streets fights at seventeen but that was it.

Ken and I reached the corner. There was a red light. I asked Ken, "What does red mean?"

"Stop," he said.

"Are you sure?" I asked. I felt like red meant go. And when it turned green I thought that I was supposed to stop.

"You better lead me," I said. I didn't want to walk into the traffic. I felt there was something courageous about suicide by car. But I didn't want to do it the same way I didn't want to shoot heroin. I was fascinated by death but I didn't want to kill myself. I was a survivor whatever my intrusive thoughts.

Ken took my elbow and led me across the street. I didn't like men touching me but I suppose it was better than death and we had been friends for years.

In the middle of the next block was his apartment. He took me upstairs. I had of course been there before.

We had a few sips of rancid wine in his kitchen. "Let's go on the roof," he said.
It was five stories up. We looked out at New York and were excited to be part of such a majestic city. The moon was full. I saw a witch flying in front of it. A goblin was throwing green cheese down at me. I felt pleasant and rotten. I thought I was in danger but I didn't know from what. I felt my brain fracturing. My logic was shivered rock.

Then I went from a fearful confused mood to a fairy dust world where everything was Neverland. Life was beautiful. I wanted to scoop the moon with my fingernails.

There was a two foot wall that surrounded the roof. Ken hopped on and started walking around. He could have fallen five stories to his death. He invited me to hop on with him. I didn't want to. But how could I not without seeming chicken. My father flew bombers in the airforce. I was meant to be brave.

I kneeled on the abutment and crawled. That was my compromise position.

I got down. "That's it," I said. "I don't take stupid chances. You want to fight, I'll fight you," I said.

"Are you crazy?" Ken said. "We are in the land of peace. We are moonshine."

I was beginning to get angry. The mescaline threw me from mood to mood like a pillow with rocks in it. I punched the wall. I didn't realize it then but I broke my pinky. That was OK. I fought off death.

Ken and I drove back in his car to his parent's house in Great Neck. We stayed up all night. I was afraid to close my eyes.

He played his latest *Doors* album. I hadn't heard them before. I obviously didn't know that Jim Morrison's life would end in tragedy. A few months in the future I would be with my schizophrenic friend Chuck in his car when we gave a lift to a hitch hiker. It was the drummer of the Doors, Ray Mancerik's, wife. She was cute. But I wasn't confident enough to try a move on a rock star's wife. Chuck was listening to voices or the radio or who knows what?

****

I am now seventy-two years old. To this day I get scared when I think back to my mescaline trip.

About twenty years later I tried pot again but it gave me hallucinations like the mescaline. The only drug that I didn't panic from was cocaine. That made me manic and I felt jumpy but not bugged out. The faster I raced the less I hallucinated.

I drank a fair amount. About ten glasses of wine a day until I kicked it in jail. I didn't want to be a loser and drink the vodka the cons sneaked in. I didn't want to fail the piss test. I didn't want to have to piss in front of the guard.

Sometimes I feel like I am losing it. Actually, I am. I am almost dead. I mean whether it's ten or thirty years makes no difference. I will be gone. I led a good life. Chuckle. No, I did. You don't learn from your mistakes. You become more yourself. And when I shake my hand I feel close to my fingers and relish the proximity of the separation.

I no longer get high. I try to stay grounded. I want to be within myself in the solidity of my own precious being. I don't want to stray from myself. I want to wander into myself and be a Warhol happening.

The Big Ski Race by the World's Greatest Senior Athlete

I had been skiing since I was six years old. It was my favorite sport. My family would take me to the Catskills or up to Vermont and I felt like I was part of my parents' lives, like we were a community of skiers. Skiing was a way to get close to my parents at a time when I was rebellious teenager who had no sense of community. I was angry. I tore myself from my family like a sheet of paper from a notebook.

I am now 72. When I look back at skiing I still get a kick out of it. Skiing was the only thing that made me feel like I should be a good kid back when I was a difficult teenager. The white snow seemed gentle and soft. I had no desire to slip into dark holes around the roots of summer trees. I was a winter boy. I hated families that went to Miami in the winter. I wanted to be in three feet of powder. I wanted to be Frosty the Snowman. I wanted to throw myself into January like a snowball.

When I was at home in Great Neck I was too busy getting in trouble and acting like a drop out. I was James Dean. I was Sal Mineo. I was trying to die young with a pretty face. I wanted to be cool. It didn't occur me that a façade was a façade was a façade. That maybe I should look for something deeper within myself.

I was often in trouble for cutting school or failing grades. But when I got into ski country I was the perfect family boy. I was proud to be with my parents. I was polite and felt like the foam in a pillow. I was snuggly. I was tight. I was restful. I avoided my negative tendencies.

Back in the sixties Americans weren't very good skiers. The Olympics were dominated by the Swiss, French and Austrians. I wasn't on an Olympic level but I made my neighbors look like snowplowing beginners.

In my twenties I went over to Chamonix to ski during Christmas vacation. I was thrilled when I skied down to the gondola and a crowd of French skiers applauded my style.

They asked me, " You American?"

"Oui," I said.

They clapped again. They were amazed that a flunky American could ski so good.
I was good. I wasn't great. I was not a racer but I could beat ninety-nine per cent of Eastern Americans.

Years later I was better than all my peers at not only skiing but at tennis and boxing. I was ranked in all three sports. I was a natural athlete. Not great but good.

And I was strong At seventy I could do 50 chin ups and one-armed dumbbell curls with fifty pounds.

I was good in everything but not good enough to be nationally known. I was ranked but not with the top players. I was something but nothing compared to champions. Well, good enough. Not many people could beat my multifarious
records. I could hold my own against people my friends couldn't compete with. I was competitive in all three sports. I wasn't good when I was a kid. I came into my prime in my late twenties and then hit a second prime in my early forties.

I didn't start ski racing until the early nineteen seventies. It seems I took up all sports a little late. In the early seventies the ski areas started a bunch of local races. They were called NASTAR races and were usually on novice hills with about thirty or so gates. They were pretty easy and when I won a few I thought I might go on to the real races in the United States Ski Racing Association.

I raced a bunch of United States Ski Association slalom and giant slalom races at Killington, Elk Mountain, Stowe, Hunter and Vernon Valley. I didn't do too well anywhere. If there were a hundred racers I would probably come in about eightieth excluding the twenty who wiped out. Once in a while by a miracle I woud come in fourth or fifth.

I didn't care about winning. It was all I could do to enter. I was proud that I was a racer. This was way above the level of NASTAR. This was not some corny, acrobatic snowboarding. This was not alpine cross-country walking through the forest.

I was the real thing, an alpine racer. I was following in the tradition of Stein Erickson, Jean Claude Killy and Karl Schranz. I was part of this fraternity of racers.

The one race that made me proud of my meagre career was held at Great Gorge in New Jersey in 1979. I drove up there from Forest Hills where I lived with my wife, Lauren.

She hated skiing. She used to go with me a little when we were dating each other. I guess she figured that I was a ski fanatic and that she had to keep my attention by occasionally going along with me. I couldn't understand why she wouldn't like the sport that I loved and that was such a familial influence on me during my teenage years. But then again she probably didn't understand why I hated balet and opera.

She decided to stop joining me when I left her in the parking lot at Hunter Mountain and told her to walk around. I headed up the mountain to enjoy some powder. When I came down at noon and found her leaning on a car she told me she never wanted to go skiing with me again. Could I blame her? No. I did.

Of course there was the time she and my son came with me to St. Moritz. We went first class all the way. She liked that. She avoided the skiing and dined by the indoor pool. She loved New Year's Eve when we dressed formally for dinner and went to a ball in the Palace Hotel. Wearing a tuxedo in ski country sickened me. It undercut the beauty of nature in the winter.

Having filled in a little backround I want to talk about the slalom race I entered at Great Gorge. My wife was home sleeping while I drove in our little BMW to the mountain.

The roads were Icey. It had rained the night before and the temperature had dropped below freezing.

At the slopes I could hardly walk to the racing preparation room without tripping. It was damned slippery.

One husky male racer said, "I'm not racing in this crap. You could get killed."

A girl said, "I'm not ruining my face on a tree."

I liked the drop outs. I figured it was to my advantage to see them disappear. Wouldn't it be wonderful if they all dropped out and I won by default?

The bibs were passed out. I was embarrassed to be stuck with "69." I hoped that didn't mean that I would end up with my face in the snow.

We went up the chairlift to the top of the slalom course. It shimmered with ice. The snow was transparent. I wondered how many of us would make it down.

I was seventh in line to go. I always loved the feeling of going into the hut and springing through the starting gate. I couldn't wait.

While I was standing in line I watched the first six racers go. All slid off the ice and crashed into slalom gates or off the course into the woods. It was like a tidal wave had washed the course clean.

The race was held up because one of the racers had broken his leg. The ski patrol took him down.

So far no one had completed the course. It was a wide-open field. I decided that I would go slow in a semi snowplow. If I could get to the bottom without falling I might win. The slower the better, the more chance of winning. I would put in the worst possible time so that I would make it through the finish line.

It was so icey that I couldn't carve a turn with my edges. I slid wide like a beginner without control. I slipped and slided. It was far from racing form.
I don't know what my time was but it was probably the slowest in the history of Great Gorge. I trembled through the finish line like an old man in a wheel chair. But I made it. I was in the number one slot.

I watched the other racers come down. They all crashed. I knew we had to do the afternoon run for me to win. The winners score was his combined races. I went to lunch and congratulated myself on being in the lead.

There were only a few racers left in the afternoon when we did our second run. This time I was first to go. I went a little faster but still didn't risk falling or crashing. I wanted to protect my lead. I slipped around the gates like I was on a surfboard.

Everyone else wiped out. I was the champ. I once knew an Irish American guy who joined the Irish team, one of the worst Olympic teams in the world. It was the only team he could qualify for. He actually won a World Cup race because of a snowstorm. I started fantasizing about joining the Israeli team. I was sure to be the best racer there. I could practice on the snow dunes and become a national hero.

The ref handed me the gold cup in the racing room. The cup read 1st place slalom, 1978, N.J.I.S.R.A. I later engraved my name on it—David Lawrence. I was proud. I was also a little embarrassed that I won because everyone else wiped out on the ice. But I was there. I finished. I won.

I got into my BMW and put my cup on the dashboard. I put on a tape and sang "Country Roads" along with John Denver. I was the happiest mediocre racer that ever lived. I couldn't wait to get home and show the gold cup to my wife. She didn't like skiing. But maybe she'd respect me. I did. I was a proud rascal.

Skiing was a sport for mountain, countryboys. It was foreign for a New York city boy to win a slalom race. I got off on the fact that I could compete with the racers when I went to museums and bought designer clothes. I was a city boy. My wife decorated our apartment with antiques. I remembered the French clapping for me at Chamonix. I thought of being in first place at Great Gorge. I thought of my wins in boxing and tennis. Perhaps I was really something. Perhaps I existed. I was autonomous. I could say that I had made it respectably through the finish line. I was not a wipe out. I was an accidental winner.

Our First Vacation

It was the summer of 1971. It was the first time that I traveled throughout Europe with my girlfriend who later became my wife. We began the trip to London and then after a week we flew to Rome. Then we flew to Tunis.

Tunis was exotic for two kids from Hunter College. My wife to be, Lauren, had seen a poster of Tunisia in a travel office and she insisted on going. We spent about ten days there before we went back to Europe. We were adventurous, particularly her. Yet she looked like a model, weighted 95 pounds and was as meek as a buttercup. She was lovely. She could have floated. It was dangerous to be with her. Every stray male stared at her. I imagined that all of Europe wanted her. I valued her and used to call her, “precious cargo.” Her mini skirt put us in danger from the swarthy Arabs.

I was wildly attracted to Lauren but didn’t really get to know her as a person until our three month European Vacation. I fell in love with her like she was a foreign country that I was exploring. I opened the doorways in her charming cities. I went down her alleyways in Amsterdam. She was suscpiciously foreign although we both were local New Yorkers.

We didn't know much about Tunis. Being Jewish, I was a little worried about how the Arabs would treat me. But we were young, naive, and willing to take chances we weren't sure existed. My wife was too pretty to have faced hostility from strangers. Ever since I was a boy I was worried that everyone would start in with me. I thought the world was like West Side Story. I had to be wary of both the Sharks and the Jets.

My wife didn't know that good looks were a temptation and could lead to her getting raped or murdered. She never had to fight against antagonists. She hadn't developed a boy's paranoia. She didn't realize that male lust could turn to violence. Most classy girls didn't know that men were dynamite just waiting to be lit. They thought we were civilized. Not that we were primitive and explosive.

This was long before 9/11 and I assumed that Arabs were non-violent, religious people. I had not heard of honor killings, female circumcisions and throwing gays off of buildings. I had not yet heard of Palestinians strapping their children to dynamite. Liberals had not yet invented Islamophobia as a dismissal of Moslem cruelty. They failed to recognize Moslem violence and blamed the victims for the terrorists. They would not admit that hating the Arabs for killing innocents was the proper form of revenge.

*****

This was also before 1993 when I attended Muslim sessions in Schuylkill Federal Prison Camp and wanted to embrace my natural enemies. In those days I thought Moslems had the inside track on doing time and I wanted to be like them. Farrakhan was a Muslim. Although he represented hatred and bigotry being friendly with Black Muslims was a form of protection in jail. I thought if I identified with the Black prisoners no one would bother to assault me. I used to line up with football player type thugs to go into prayer meetings. The cleric would announce me at the meetings, "Now here is David, a Jew, who is curious enough to attend our meetings. We should respect him."

I attended the Jewish meetings too. But they didn't care. They didn't understand self-protection. They didn't understand that Jews should be warriors not forgiving liberals. They should be hard Israelis not blind-folded progressives.

*****

In Tunis we stayed at the Maison Doree. The name was fancier than the hotel but it wasn't bad. Particularly, on a student's budget. We ate at outdoor cafes where my wife was the only woman. It was an all male society. My wife wore sexy outfits. She could have gotten us killed. I remonstated with her but she hadn't brought any long skirts on the trip.

After a few days in Tunis we took a taxi down to Gabes near the Sahara desert. We passed through an alternate world. We saw donkeys, olive trees, sheep, rams and Arabs in clothes that wandered around them like loose sails. We passed huts, camels and donkeys. We went by a Roman Aqueduct. I felt like I was Lawrence of Arabia. Maybe I was Peter O'Toole. Maybe I was a movie star.

We finally arrived at the Hotel Oasis. Arabs in khaki suits took our bags up the marble steps. We checked into this luxurious palace for ten dollars a night. The dollar was good. The dollar was strong. We could buy the world.

The next day we took a bus to Douz. From there we all rode camels. My wife had a particularly fast one and raced ahead of me.

The next day we went to Matmata. The people lived in little caves. After lunch I made a big mistake. I left My wife alone while I went back on the camel for a ride without her. I couldn't resist going out again like I couldn't resist taking more ski runs at Hunter Mtn. while I left my wife in the parking lot.

While I was carelessly gone on my camel I later found out that the guide offered to take my wife around the caves. When he was in a remote corner he held my wife's hand and tried to kiss her. He told her he had never seen someone as beautiful as her. No doubt. Most of the Arab women were ugly and veiled.

My wife was too innocent to lead the guide on and ran outside away from the lech. Soon she saw me coming back on my camel. I was wearing a headwrap and my wife later told me that I looked like an Arab sheik.

On the bus back to Tunis my wife told me what had happened with the guide. She made sure that he sensed that she had told me and gave him a dirty look. He twitched and looked nervous.

I was caught somewhere between being frightened and that I might have to kill him and spend the rest of my life in a Tunisian jail.

I felt that it was an insult to myself not to murder him. But I knew I wouldn't get a fair trial against an Arab in Tunisia.

I thought of Meursault in "L'Etrangere" and how he was executed for killing an Arab.

And yet I had to do something to defend My wife's honor. I was ashamed of my dithering.

When I was a teenager the guide wouldn't have gotten away with this. I would have punched him in the face and pulled his ear off. He'd be dead as a run over deer on the road.

College had made me soft. And my psychiatrist in high school. I had become a pacifist. There is no pride in cowardice. Yet I couldn't bring myself to hit him. I should have killed him.

Back at the Hotel Oasis we went swimming in the Mediterranean. I'm shy and don't like to dance and don't like to fight publicly but that night I danced with my wife. She's the best dancer I ever saw. I'd just imitate her steps and we'd look like Astaire and Rogers, except she was leading.

In the morning we were scheduled to take a taxi back to Tunis. It took us five hours. This time we checked in at the Majestic Hotel instead of the Maison D'Oree. It was a little classier.

The next morning we waved goodbye to the exotic landscape and caught a plane to Rome. I felt like a failed gladiator. I was Woody Allen in an absent helmet. I should have killed that Hotel guide. I would have been a real man, not someone who apologized for being a victim.

After Rome we took a train up to Vienna. My wife got sick in a small town in the Alps, Tarvisio, and we spent a week there while she recuperated. Then we went to Paris, Amsterdam, London and finally New York.

We both wore headwraps as my dad picked us up at the airport. We held hands in the back seat.

I was in love with my wife. I regretted having to leave her when my dad dropped her off with her parents in Forest Hills.

The following weekend we went out to Montauk. My grandfather had bought a house there on the lake. We wore white embroidered shirts we bought in Tunis. We took part of Tunisia with us. We were the atmosphere of the desert without the heat.

We were international travelers. But sometimes countries were at war. I wished that I had killed that guide who has harassed my wife. It would have meant that I stood up for something. That I was not an unprincipled, progressive weakling. Which I was at that time. Long, long ago before I identified with Robert Frost's, "Good fences make good neighbors." The title of that poem is "Mending Wall." It's in the mending the bifurcation that we mend the lives that were destroyed by separation and insane diversity.

It's only in the humane sameness that we accept the differences without celebrating them.

On Not Buying A Yacht

In 1981 I went with my wife to the boat show at the Coliseum. It was on the west side of Manhattan. I was not a sailor. But my wife liked classy stuff like yachts and Rolls Royces. I did too. But I disliked my superficiality. We eventually bought an upper east side coop and a Rolls.

I was born on the upper west side of New York City in 1947 when it was poor. I didn't like it even if I didn't understand it. It was pre-Hippy. It was casual and the people were recovering fromWorld War II. Everyone was trying to find his way, to build careers.

This was before my Great Neck years in the sixties when life became throwback-hippy. It was all floral shirts and corduroys. It was rich people pretending that they were trashy. It was faux intellectuals and naïve socialists. I didn't wear a beard. I wasn't rumpled. I wasn't a slob. Not that I wore a tuxedo. But I washed my hair.

I was more formal than Columbus Avenue where I was born. I was upper East Side—Madison Avenue. I was a museum not an opium den. I was an antique store amongst the rich. I was the art show at the Armory on Park Avenue and the Sixties. I was polite, elgant and discrete. I turned my nose at the west side Colliseum.

I was at the boat show with my wife, who was precious and expensive. She was in the society crowd. We never really thought about buying a yacht but we figured we'd take a look. Remember these were the days of millionaires not billionaires. People were formal unlike the t-shirted computer nerds who dominate in the twenty-first century. I had money to burn but I could not start a barnfire.

We were somewhat impressed by the modest yachts. There was nothing that large there but there were plenty of thirty and forty footers with interior cabins, kitchens and bathrooms. There were no Adnan Khashog or Donald Trump yachts. The boats were not fabulous but they were upper middle class. I could see myself walking the deck in a blue blazer and toasting my wife with champagne. I could be Bing Crosby in Connecticut.

There was one Hatteras yacht that was going for six hundred thousand dollars. That kind of appealed to me except that I knew that I had a tendency to sea sickness. I even got car and bus sick. Why would I want to dally with travel sickness? It made no sense. For some reason I always leaned towards things that were wrong for me.

I wanted to climb Mt. Everest even though I was afraid of heights. Maybe it would make sense for me to buy a yacht even though I got sea sick? Maybe it would make sense for my lungs to burst on the top of the Himalyas?

I thought of the time when I was first dating my wife to be, and we took a boat from Yugoslavia to Venice. I was nauseous the whole time. My legs were jittery and doing a dance while I sat on a deck chair on the boat. Later on in life I would realize that the twinges were like neuropathy. In my early seventies my toes got the jitters and the tingles from having spent so many years on my feet. It reminded me of that boat trip.

My wife and I discussed the Hatteras. We both were luke warm. We had recently checked out a house in Westhampton and realized that we couldn't afford both. It was either the house or the boat.

We decided on the house which was a bargain at three hundred thousand dollars. It was on Quarter Court Road and had both a swimming pool and a har-tru tennis court.

After buying it in cash, I let my wife go to work decorating it beautifully. She had fabulous taste. Maybe not in men but who knows? Maybe I was better than I thought. Maybe I was the sweetest brassard hound in the kennel. She was the most elegant greyhound. We licked each other so that we could taste love's meal. We were delicious. We were a cute couple. We were pretty.

The second year I bought a Kawasaki three-wheeler and a Yamaha Enduro bike and kept them in Westhampton. My son, Graham, was four years old and my wife intelligently wouldn't let him sit on the bikes with me.

I used to ride over to the motocross track about two miles from my house early in the morning before the real riders showed up. I would ride around the course with the twelve year olds.

They were chaperoned by their fathers. I was their fathers' ages but none of the old men were riding.

I would wear garish outfits with bright decals, a lime green helmet and yellow pants with knee pads. I had so much padding on that I looked like the ghostbusters blimp in the Macy's Day Parade. A neighbor asked me if I just arrived from Mars?

My fellow riders' fathers eyed me suspiciously like I was some sort of nut or pervert.

It so happened around this time that our young Greek driver was driving his motorcycle on the Grand Central Parkway and that he got hit by a truck and died. My wife knew this ahead of me.

She got a phone call while I was in the garage warming up my bikes. My son and wife came out to the garage crying and told me that I had to stop riding, "Jerry was killed on his motorcycle."

I didn't know what to say. I liked Jerry.

I said, "Alright, I'll give up my motorcycles. But I'm taking up boxing."

"Fine," My wife said.

I didn't really mean it. I had no interest in boxing. But when my wife agreed to my proposition I decided to do it. The next day I signed up at Gleason's Gym. I never left it. Thirty years later I now realize that my boxing had ruined my short term memory. I also get confused easily and sometimes think I see faces I don't know but recognize remotely. I get lost in my own neighborhood. Maybe motorcycling would have inflicted less damage.

I miss the motorcycle wheelies. It was a rush like ski racing. Boxing is so much more like walking into a thud, wiping my face in a sponge. It is not flying. It is being knocked down. I remember getting knocked out cold in my first pro fight in Denver. The Doctor woke me with his flashlight in my eyes. I didn't know where I was or who I was. I smiled. It was a dumb smile. It was a lost giggle.

Maybe I should have bought that yacht. It might have been safer. Then maybe again I would have drowned. I'm not a great swimmer.

I look forward to seeing my neurologist this week. I'm not sure if he thinks I am faking. I don't really know if I have a taste of dementia or the beginnings of alzheimers.

I also have to see my psychiatrist. He has been treating me for bipolar disease for twenty years. I don't know what I am or am not. Is that the consequence of not having bought the yacht? I am sailing through life celebrating myself. Eveything I do is a song. Although I hate music. The notes hurt my ability to concentrate. They hurt my focus. I am introspective. I do not like to be distracted.

New Year's at St. Moritz

My wife was never a big ski fan. Ever since I dumped her in the parking lot at Hunter Mountain she had no desire to go skiing with me. It's not that I meant to be rude but I was such a ski fanatic that I couldn't wait to get up to the top of the mountain by myself. I ignored her. It was not nice. But I was mountain obsessed.

While my wife was not into skiing she was into glitz. So when her friends, the Cohens, told her they were going with their son to the Palace Hotel in St. Moritz, my wife decided that she could do with a little skiing. It appealed to her sense of snobbery. The Palace was old world, new world luxury. It was royalty. It was a castle floating in the Alps.

I myself had skied in Zermatt, Chamonix and Innsbruck. I had also skied at St. Moritz in college when I was at Hunter. So this was not my first trip there. But back then I didn't realize its elegance. It was a college ski trip so we stayed in some dumpy youth hostel. All the other students were impressed by my skiing. I had been skiing most of my life. I was an expert and most of them were rank beginners.

This time we didn't stay at a youth hostel but at the Palace Hotel which was one of the ritziest hotels in the world. It was movie land. I could imagine James Bond or David Niven walking around in tuxedos. It was the playland of millionaires in the eighties.
The Cohen's brought their six-year-old son, Aaron, along and we brought our son, Graham, with us.

We shared a suite with the Cohen's overlooking a lake with a view of the mountains. Kenny was a big-time decorator in New York. So was his wife, Penny. He was gay and I couldn't figure out why they were married. There were rumors that Penny had been impregnated by their neighbor in East Hampton.

This was before gay pride became de rigeur and Kenny and his wife used to sneak around pretending that they were a happily married couple.

Some people said that Penny married him because he was a better decorator and she wanted to work with him and share his reputation. They were pretty prominent but not big time. Their rooms weren't displayed in the major, glossy magazines. No Architectural Digest or Architectural Review.

I don't think they ever went out skiing. But I took my wife and Graham out on some of the novice slopes. My wife found them too difficult and had me take her back to the hotel. Graham and I went out again and he skied most of the day with me. I held him on his little skis between my legs as we coasted down the mountain.

On New Year's Eve we had to dress formally to dinner. This was the first time that I had to carry my tuxedo across half of the world to wear in the evening. I hated it. But I had to do what I had to do. Women control the social events. My wife was my high-class coach. She was also the decorator of my home and the glue in our marriage.

If I could follow my own whims I would probably have been a ski instructor. I loved skiing. When I was first dating my wife I almost left her for a job ski bumming at Jackson Hole. When she told me she didn't mind if I left, I decided to stay. I was annoyed at how casual she was about my leaving.

One afternoon both of our families rented a horse drawn sleigh driven by a valet and went a few hundred yards from the Palace Hotel and had a picnic. The basket was filled with sandwhiches, fruits and wine. It was delicious. I felt like I was in a Sonya Henny film in the mountains. It was upper class. It was formal yet rustic.

In the evening we left our children in our suite with a maid and went out for an evening of festivities.

I felt like I was on the outer rim of the high class. All the men were dressed like maîtred's and the women were wearing designer evening gowns. A lot of diamonds sprinkling the necks of the women. My wife was draped in chunky emeralds. Kenny wore a sapphire earing. Penny wore a casual Indian necklace.

We danced before, while and after dinner. I felt that I had landed at Buckingham Palace and was part of the Queen's formal party. Class was as class does and we participated in the elegance. We were snowflakes come in from the slopes floating under vast ceilings.

About one o'clock in the morning we came back to our room. We tipped the maid. Our son was asleep but Penny's son Aaron was crying. He missed his mommy.

Kenny told him to shut up. When he didn't he picked him up and threw him down on the bed and scolded him like a mad woman.

"Leave the kid alone" I told Kenny.

"He's mine. I can do what I want," he said.

I probably should have punched him in the face but I didn't want to end up in a Swiss jail, not that I could imagine it being too rough.

Instead I went down to the concierge and told him that we wanted our own suite and didn't want to board with the Cohen's any longer. I was lucky that they had one suite left. It was larger. It was even more expensive but it was worth it to get away from Kenny.

The concierge asked, "When do you want to move?"

"Right now," I said.

"I'll send the porter up in ten minutes," the concierge said.

I went back upstairs and whispered to my wife. She approved of my decision. I then told Kenny and Penny that we are moving to our own suite because this is too crowded.

They didn't put up a fight even though it added another five hundred dollars a night to our stay and theirs. Maybe they didn't want me around when they abused their son? Could they have been ashamed?

The next day my son had whooping cough and sat around the heated pool with his mother.

I went to out ski. I skied double black diamonds at full tilt. I didn't want what I had seen to catch up with me. Kenny was a trail of disgust.

I had to escape Kenny's child abuse. I didn't want the ugliness to spread onto my face. I didn't want to be part of Kenny's sickness. I did not want to be pimpled with his cruelty.

I was a good father, I was, I was. I didn't want to be involved in his family's sickness.

I joined my wife and son at the pool. I sunk into the luxury of the heat rising from the water. I hoped I never had to see Kenny again.

His resentment towards his son turned the luxury of the Palace Hotel into the perversion of a twisted mind.

I thought of the sickness of his family and I felt pretty good about mine. Cruelty even infects beautiful places like the Alps. Anger and perversion are loss leaders.
To hit a child like Kenny did was to hit at the soul of the innocent universe. It was to turn a fluffy snowball into ice.

The Cancer Dance

My wife dragged me to the cancer dance. It was sponsored by the American Society for Cancer. It was one of the numerous charities that we went to when we were rich. Now that I lost my business and had been in jail, we only went out on occasion. We contributed as little as possible. The state had taken my humdrum career from me. I didn't feel like giving anything to anyone.

We'd also spent some time at Meals-on-Wheels. We liked the chefs. And of course, the cause there, AIDS, was *de rigeur* at Meals. It seemed a bit ironic to go to parties for tragic situations. I didn't really want to party-hardy for diseases.
I didn't particularly care about AIDS. I mean I wasn't gay and I wasn't going to get it. Selfishness is self-preservation and I looked over my back to make sure I wasn't getting shafted. I hated goody goodies who pretended that they cared about all their neighbors. I was a prick. So I was a prick. I was large. I did what I wanted.

Now that I had lost my fortune I felt even more distressed about attending glitzy charity parties. I didn't feel a generous bone in my body despite my earlier gifts to the unfortunate. I felt I could be a chairitable cause rather than a contributer. I had lost more than most people. I was a deficit without hope. I hadn't worked in years. I was a loss leader who was no longer capable of leading.

I hated charities. I hated dressing up. I didn't care about good causes. I didn't believe that there were any good causes that worked and these meetings were just ways for rich people to feel good about themselves. Some of the people who threw these parties stole money from them. Who knows how many needy people actually got their money? The Clintons were known for grabbing money from their Haitian charity. I met a Yugoslavian princess who lived off her charities.

I felt good about myself regardless of my forced cheapness just because I never let anything get me down. In jail I was happy to work out and write poetry. I identified with felons not benefactors. I couldn't buy happiness. Contributing to charities meant nothing to me and I could no longer afford it. Generosity was not my game. I didn't chose to play at that level.

Naming the sadness of cancer the "cancer dance" was an abomination. Cancer was pain. It was not jubiliation. I didn't want to dance to cancer as if it were a party.

I particularly hated when I had to wear a tuxedo. In fact I never liked wearing formal clothes. Not even when I was rich. I thought that men looked like penguins in their tuxedos. I felt cold like I was in the Arctic.

We husbands were all lap dogs in collars leashed to our wives. I didn't like the gambling—the cards, the roulette and the slots. I felt my luck was running bad just because I had to be there. I never won at anything. I lost most of my money when I lost my business and went to jail. Here I lost my chips.

I was a loser who didn't have to give away money to feel good about myself. I didn't like being generous just to be generous about my feelings about myself. I didn't particularly like me. In fact my distaste for myself made me kind of respect and like myself.

I wish my wife didn't drag me to these places. It seems that most of the men who weren't gay came here because of their wives. I used to go to the Cancer Dance when I was rich. Now that I was here without a real job I felt out of place. I had no money, nothing to give, nowhere to hide, nwhere to run. What was I? A boxing coach among millionaires.

Women love to show themselves off. They dress up and try to look good. I don't care how I look. I'm good looking but who cares? I think appearance is superficial. I am a poet. I want to get lost in the wonderlust of words. I want to feel life and death. I want to juggle them. I want to die of cancer and live through my optamism. Why would I celebrate something that would probably eventually kill me? A lot of cancer ran in my family. Their skeletons weren't dancing.

Cancer is real. It is deadly. But a cancer dance is a mockery of the tragedy of cancer. My mother and father both died of cancer. My grandmother died of cancer when she was fifty. My uncle died of cancer when he was twenty-five. Chemo hardly helped. It was an elicitor of vomit. Death took little pieces out of them with its spoon.

The thing about the cancer dance is that the charity lets you write off all your gambling debts. In the old days when I had money we substituted debts for gifts from Cartier and Tiffany's and reduced them from our taxes. That was fun. We considered our losses contributions. I got a ten thousand dollar Panther watch for a tax deduction in the old days. Afterall it was for charity. That was then. Now I bought popcorn. There were no deductions for kernals.

Years later I went to jail for two years for tax evasion. No one understands how I liked jail. What do I know? I am what I am. Once again I'm Popeye the sailor man. I didn't let jail beat me down. I didn't want to let the authorities conquer my spirit. I made jail into my own space. I wrote and worked out five hours a day.

Some of my wife's and my old friends were at the Cancer Dance. I said hello to Kenny, the gay decorator who had a phoney marriage to Penny. He was wearing a tuxedo with a pink cowboy tie. He had ruffles on his sleeves and was wearing multi-colored cowboy boots. He was the creep who roughed up his son at St. Moritz when we were on vacation there.

Stevie was trying to look rich. He actually was rich but not super rich. He was more like me before I lost m business—flashy. To live up to his nouveau rich image he wore a creased hundred dollar bill in place of a pocket hankie.

Barbara was there. She wore a berqa to identify with America's enemies. She was Jewish. She would have stepped into a concentration camp oven if it showed her generoisity and ability to identify with her enemies. She thought it was Islamophobic to hate the murderers who knocked down the World Trade Center. One thousand more dead at Ground Zero than in Pearl Harbor and she was worried about being rude to a Moslem cab driver. She claimed she wanted to go to the Rain Forest to help the rain. Her Forest Green Ungarro dress could have fed a village.

A couple of dead people on the southern border and now AOC compares it to the killing of six million Jews in Nazi Germany. She doesn't blame any of the coyotes for the deaths.

Where has all proportion gone? Long time passing.

Years ago I used to contribute to charity. Not because I was generous but because I had to keep up with the Schwartz's. My charity was actually to my image as a charitable person.

But when I went to jail for two years for tax evasion I stopped all charitable giving. I figured the government had confiscated all my money. I was one of the deprived. Why should I be generous? I was no fool. I had boxed for years. When someone hit me I hit them back. I didn't give them a gift. Screw my enemies. I would not be fool enough to turn the other cheek.

A dance for cancer is oxymoronic tomfoolery. It is like throwing coins in a homeless man's cup. Ironically, I once did a modeling job for the MTA. The poster said you shouldn't give charity to the homeless but you should get them into treatment programs. This add ran for seven years in every subway train in the city. It read, "He may be without a home,but he's not without help."

I was photographed as a homeless man. I seemed what I was not. I hated what I posed for. I liked the homeless in the nineteen-fifties when you only ran into one about three hours. Now there's one on every subway car and every corner. They've become a nuisance.

Don't crowd me in with the real homeless. If I were really homeless I would know my place. If I had cancer I wouldn't dance. I would be sick. I would try to adjust to my death.

Coming back to the Cancer Dance with my wife made me feel out of place. This time around I wasn't giving. I had nothing to give. I had nothing to feel good about. A lot of my family had had cancer. I felt bad for them. I wasn't in the mood for dancing. Well, at least I didn't have cancer. That was nice.

THE CAR

It was a night like any other night in New York City. I was alone in the back seat of my Rolls Royce. My driver Michael was driving me downtown. I don't remember where. Time is the repetitive shops on 1st Avenue. There are no bargains. We die in the corners of buildings.

Time squeezed into itself and me. It congested itself outside my car windows. My feet lay on the black carpet like a wad of hundred dollar bills. I was richly comfortable.

I was in my large black car made more lonely by the fact that I was financially superior to most of the people I passed in the streets and many of the cars. Did they hate me or admire me? Did I give them a lift? Did I enter their dreams?
Was I a beautiful museum that pedestrians could gaze upon and see the art of riches? A Ferrari was a sexy sports car. A Rolls Royce was a coffin for elderly rich people.

I was always in my Silver Spur. At least before 1993 when I went to jail and I had to return my car to the dealer. I remember telling the dealer, "Here. I'm giving this beauty back." I felt like I was breaking up with a girlfriend.

He said, "You can't. Your car is on a lease."

I told him that I am going to jail and I might as well just leave the car in the street because I have no more money to pay for it. He took the Rolls back and I got a cab on the corner.

Michael was a proper driver. He was one of my many drivers who included Said, Raj and him. He only spoke to me when I spoke to him. I liked him even though my wife had accused him of stealing from us. She even said that he would bring his girlfriend's laundry into our cleaners and charge the bill to us.

I didn't care. I didn't take much seriously. He was a reliable driver even if he stole a few dollars from me here and there. As long as he drove us from location to location safely he was alright in my books.

Michael was Israeli. He was in the paratroopers. I figured that meant that he was tough. He used to watch me box in the mornings at Gleason's Gym. When he challenged me to box I was a little surprised and afraid. However, I knew he had no experience at boxing and I boxed six days a week. Was he kidding? We were friends. What the heck?

In the morning Sammy the Bull Gravano used to work out with a trainer at Gleasons who wouldn't dare hit him. Michael became buddies with Gravano's driver. It was kind of fun for him feeling like he was hanging out with the mob. I didn't want to take chances with Gotti's crew.

Michael was about one hundred and ninety pounds. I was one forty- seven. But when the bell rang I discovered he had no defense. I dropped him twice in the first round and he saw that he needed some experience to fight me. He was a tough guy but I was training to be a professional boxer.

The next day he called in sick. Apparently my punches had caused some blood in his kidneys. He took two days off. I used my car services—Communicar and Concord. They didn't have Rolls Royce's. Only Lincolns. I was proud of how I had injured Michael. I was impressed by myself. I thought maybe I should join the Israeli army.

I liked having a driver who I had fought. There was a certain comradery about having gone through something hurtful together.

I don't remember every place we went that night. It was thirty years ago, before I lost my business, went to jail and became a boxing instructor.

I had the air of a tuxedo. I was formal. I was gorgeous. This was before I wandered the subways in crinkled jeans after losing my insurance business and becoming one of the people.

I told Michael to go down to Café Society. My wife liked the place. I figured I'd just get a bite to eat with Michael. I liked that I would hang out with my driver and some of my boxing buddies. They loved driving in the Rolls. I wasn't slumming. I was expanding. It was kind of sad trying to hang out with my chauffeur. Lonely is five card poker using only four cards. My luck was winding down. My multimillion dollar business was failing. I had let it run amuck while I was concentrating on boxing and raping.

When we got down to Café Society I told Michael I changed my mind. I wanted to go home. I wanted to see my wife.

I was lonely. Michael couldn't fill the void. I could hang out with my chauffeur but I couldn't feel it was meaningful. I needed a woman who was part of me. I wanted Lauren.

We turned around at Union Square and headed back up town. I didn't want to be out in the world. I looked at the sidewalks and watched the good looking girls waving at me.

But they didn't know me. I felt used. They wanted to be part of the world where a nice looking guy was in a Rolls Royce.

They were the opposite of my rich friends. My friend Jeff who was the son of the richest man in the insurance industry, used to make me pick him up two blocks from one of his buildings because he didn't want any of his employees seeing him in a Rolls Royce. He was embarrassed by such ostentation. He thought my car was tacky. Maybe he was right but it sure had a priceless, artistic presence. No one knew that as a side venture he owned the largest jet leasing firm in the world.
Passing the stylish women, I was the sight of the century, the attention grabber, the youngish, smooth executive who was on the cover of *American Health Magazine*. There was even a five page article on me in *People Magazine*. Not to mention *New York Magazine*. I did a half hour segment on the *Phil Donohue Show*.

I had the world by the brass balls. I palmed them like I was about to toss dice. Sometimes life is craps.

I made wagers on my unhappiness and sat in my car like I was in a priceless museum, feeling isolated.

I was lonely. I don't know why. I had my paid help, Michael, driving me around. He was company. I wanted to talk to him but I didn't talk much.

I thought that the girls on the sidewalks were waving at the car not at me. I didn't even want to wave at me. I was the surface failure of ambition tripping over its own feet. And yet I hated success and hated business.

The women wanted me because they didn't know me. If they knew me they'd know that I was a ball of narcissism on a tennis court with broken racquet strings.

I was a distraction not an attraction. And I was a Rolls Royce disappearing down a vanishing avenue Into a leased night.

When I got home I felt good when the doorman let me out of my Rolls Royce. I was a success. I was a failure. I was the happiness that unhappiness trampled upon. I was failed chemistry. I was inexplicable depression when I wasn't manic self-interest. I hadn't yet been told that I was bipolar. That's too bad. I would have avoided some of my mistakes. I wouldn't have committed tax evasion just for fun but because I would eventually need the money. I wouldn't have wallowed in cash just because I thought it was more gangster. I wouldn't have done everything wrong because it was more fun than doing it right.

Jail Rebirth

I was running my insurance wholesale brokerage back in the eighties and early nineties. It was mostly legit but sometimes we'd play games to milk more profit out of it. I had a real estate account, *Madison Equities*, that I made ten times the profit I should have made on it. I didn't know this. It was engineered by my senior vice president, Kelly. I wasn't paying too much attention to what my employees did. I was busy in the gym training for my boxing bouts and in the studio doing rap songs.

I was doing rap albums. I was a real dilettante. I did everything well but nothing super-great. Yet I was written about in almost every newspaper and magazine in America, Germany and England. I guess it was odd for a Ph.D., millionaire businessman to want to get his head beaten in in pro boxing. Was I self-destructive or looking for some sort of notice or attention? Was I guilty for reasons I couldn't figure out? Did Ilove and hate myself at the same time?

As an insurance wholesaler my diem would get a quote out of the insurance underwriter and deliver it to the insured's broker. Kelly was the best at this. By lying about the loss experience he managed to get fifty buildings insured for property casualty for fifty thousand dollars. The insurance company should have gotten seven hundred thousand dollars. Instead my office grabbed the seven hundred thousand and paid the insurance company a lousy fifty thousand. We then quoted it out at seven hundred thousands dollars to the broker and his insured. We kept the six hundred and fifty thousand dollars difference.

When my employee Kelly told me that our profit on Madison Equities was six hundred and fifty thousand dollars, I was shocked. That was the difference between the underwriters quote and the number we delivered to the broker. The average commission on this account would have been a mere seventy thousand dollars. With my staggering overhead on Wall Street I had to make a lot more than a few thousand dollars to sustain my company. So I let Kelley run wild to my benefit.

I asked Kelley why the underwriter was willing to write the account for a lousy premium of fifty thousand dollars.

He said, "That's all the company wanted. What was I to do? Give away your money boss?"

I told him that I thought another company might do it for less than the seven hundred thousand that we were charging to the client?

"Who?" he asked. "The losses stink."

"Then how'd you get the price down so low?"

"The money. The pay off."
"What pay off?"

"I delivered thirty thousand dollars in hundred dollar bills in a suit case to the underwriter at a restaurant. We snorted a few lines of coke in the men's room to celebrate our monetary high. I introduced him to a girl that I knew."

Underwriters were easy to pay off. They controlled billions of dollars of exposure and were ripe targets for brokers. They all made mediocre salaries and the brokers made much more money than the underwriters. They could pay for good quotes.

"We could go to jail," I said. "The spread is too obvious. You need a sense of proportion."

"What's done is done," Kelly said. "I'll need the thirty grand back."

It was done well. I was making an inordinate profit. Kelly did all the stealing. I was just the behind the scenes guy. My only cost was the underwriter and Kelly. I'd buy him a new car or pay for the hormone shots for his male lover's sex change operation. I'd also pay him back the thirty grand he gave the underwriter from petty cash.

I felt insulated from the pay off by Kelly. He was doing all the bribery. They couldn't even trace me back to the crime. Kelly did the pay off and I got the big profit. No reason the feds should come after me when Kelly was obviously the front man.

Life imitates art. My life had become *Dog Day Afternoon.* Kelly needed money to pay for his boyfriend's sex change. He actually committed the bribery and the engineering of my company's making enormous profits. I felt if the law got involved I might not be noticed.

For every Madison Equities there were ten other accounts that I was glomming money off. I had turned a small insurance brokerage into a gold mine. Instead of making ten percent commissions I was keeping ninety per cent of the premium.

It's ironic that I was never caught for stealing all this money. I was caught instead for some stupid tax evasion again engineered by Kelley. Apparently, Kelly was taking hundreds of thousands of dollars and sending it down to some of his gay friends in Delaware.

To keep the Feds from catching on, Kelly had his gay crowd cash all the money in amounts under ten thousand dollars to duck the Feds. It seems I had a hundred bank accounts in Delaware. I had never even been to Delaware. I was a dupe rather than a brainy criminal.

Insurance was a nickel and dime business unless you stole from the premiums to jack up on the commissions. I was eventually nailed for tax evasion. The cash we were stealing from the pemiums were not getting recorded.
I didn't know much about this but as the president of Allied Programs I was held responsible. The feds nailed me and I went to jail for two years. I needed a vacation. I got along well in jail. I was a boxer and a rapper. I was a bit special.

After sixteen months in Schuykill Federal Prison Camp, they sent me back to halfway house in New York for five months. I cried when leaving jail. I felt secure there. Everything was taken care of for me. I didn't know what I had left for me at home. I didn't know if my wife would take me back and if I had a job. No, I knew I didn't have a job.

I thought I'd write a bunch of books. I had been writing my whole life. I looked forward to the words. I recreated myself within myself and felt closer to myself than I had ever felt before. I was reborn through jail. I locked myself up within myself and looked at myself through an invisible mirror.

Pops at Schuylkill Federal Prison Camp

For my quasi tax evasion I was assigned to Schuylkill Federal Prison Camp. Actually, I bought my way in there by paying a prison counselor five grand to put me in an easy facility not too far from home. It was in the Poconos, about a three hour drive from New York.

I was worried that as a wussy tax evader I wouldn't get the respect of a meth or heroin dealer. Wherever I went I wanted to be the best. I wanted to be a real dyed in the wool criminal. I fantasied about the lethal injection. I wanted to take it to prove that I was tough. I'd been knocked out in the ring. I wasn't afraid to be obliterated by a needle. Don't fuck with me. I just don't care.

I was hoping they would put me on the chain gang. But there were no chain gangs in a minimum security prison. That was movie stuff. Punishment that weaklings cried over to feel like they were good people.

I had already spent a million dollars on my lawyer Ben Brafman and his crew. I didn't even know if I was guilty of tax evasion. I believe it was my two vice presidents who were stealing from me and the government. But as the president of Allied Programs Corp I had to take the bullet for what my flunkies were doing.

I was in my dorm at Prison Camp about six months when I saw a guard walking a little old man down the aisle, two units past mine. He looked like he belonged in a nursing home rather than a prison. He shuffled like he had cuffs on his feet, even though he didn't.

He was wearing a khaki uniform because he probably didn't have enough money for his own clothes. He had on prison steel toe boots.

I wondered what the heck? What could this little old man be doing in jail? He couldn't have mugged someone or raped a woman.

The guard introduced him to the dorm, "This is pops." The jail system had to be kidding. It was wasting forty thousand dollars a year to keep this old codger in jail.

I guess the guards liked him. He was easy to handle. Better than a killer.

The old man was lucky to get his own cubicle with the double decker bunk. If there was another prisoner already in the cubicle he would have been forced to climb up to the top bunk because the bottom bunk is based on seniority.

I liked pops. For no reason. He was different than your usual criminal. He reminded me of a senile version of my dead grandpa.

I could see that some of the hard-core bikers didn't like him much. They felt jail should be for tough guys, not old men. I wondered what I would do if these baldy bikers started in with Pops. Would I have the balls to protect him? Or was I just a guy who was tough in the boxing ring but wouldn't stand up to help an old man?
I needed ropes and rules to play by. I didn't like the vagueness of street fights. Even though I had a number of them when I was a kid.

When I was out of jail I thought about Pops and missed my jail days. I mean it wasn't only him who was interesting. I missed some of the mafia guys. I'd watch these fatties cooking spaghetti and meatballs on their hot plates after dinner. They looked like they couldn't beat up their sisters. They'd need a gun. I weighed a hundred and forty-five pounds, was over educated and rich and could probably beat them all up. They were probably about as tough as a dried out steak.

The drug dealers were usually thin. They looked like they had done too much coke in their lives. We had one midget computer hacker. He was a real nerd. But he was famous and there were constantly reporters coming up to interview him.

There were a few slugs there for breaking and entering, car theft and low class crimes. Also some guys running private gambling rings.

Pops was there on welfare fraud. I didn't know what that was but I guess that he stole some checks from the government. Nothing like my million dollars on tax evasion. He was small potatoes. In fact, he slumped around like Mr. Potato Head.
The first night I noticed that Pops had a problem making it from the dorm to the urinal. He would piss on the floor.

One of the bikers said, "You do that again and I'll stick your nose in your own puddle like a dog."

He didn't.

But if he did what would I have done?

I wasn't looking for trouble. I didn't want to get into some kind of gang fight. I didn't want to get stabbed. Stabbings were rampant in jail. Every few hours a whistle would blow over at the Medium Security Prison which was right next door to the camp and convicts would be sent back to their cells because someone had been stabbed.

Would I have punched the biker? Or would I have punked out and made fun of sweet old Pops barking like a dog?

Was I a good person? I doubt it. Afterall I had been in jail. But I knew people on the outside who were mean like the bikers. The human brain is in my heart. It beats with love regardless of my circumstances. I would never hurt the old man. But would I protect him? There's the rub upon which I evaluated myself.

To defend or not to defend. That was the question. Was I Hamlet or just a person without values? Was I trapped in ambivalent, adolescent indecision? Did I know myself? Or was I constantly being reintroduced to myself? Did I look the other way?

Separate Rooms

I had been out of jail for five years and I had been living with my parents. We lived on Seventy-Second street and 1st Avenue and Lauren and my son, Graham, lived on Madison and Seventy-Second.

Every morning I would wake up early and meet Graham at seven o'clock for breakfast before he went to school. I think I was a good father, despite jail. I don't know what he thinks.

I would see Lauren one to two nights a week for dinner. It seems that I got along better with her only seeing her intermittently. It was like we were dating again instead of being married. It was more casual. It was kind of young and romantic.

My mother died from cancer in 1999 just before the millennial. My dad sold their apartment and moved to Del Ray in Florida. There was no place for me to stay anymore unless I lived with my dad to Florida.

My wife, wanting to keep me in and out of her life, invited me back to her building. She wanted me closer to her than Florida. My son had graduated from Columbia and moved down to Battery Park so his room was open.

I moved back in with Lauren. She wanted me to get a real job but I kept ducking the question. Instead I took acting classes, did modeling jobs and taught boxing at Gleason's Gym.

I did the modeling partially to impress my wife. I was surprised when I did fairly well. I did a commercial with Anna Kornikova, a picture with Donna Mills for *Town and Country*, an add for *Men's Health* and a cover for *American Health.* Over the years I also starred in feature articles for *People Mag., New York Mag., Men's Journal, Time Out, The New York Times, The Post, The Daily News, Stern and Kraftwerk.*

There were many others jobs I don't remember. I gave up trying to act when I landed a role as a detective in a Russian television show and I discovered that I couldn't remember the lines. I had partial brain damage from years of boxing.

I also did standup comedy, published a thousand poems in good magazines and rapped three albums. Not to mention a popular jazz album in London on Polygram that I did with Nina Simone's brother—Sam Waymon.

Out of all my glitzy projects I made practically no money. The only thing that paid at all was the boxing coaching. My wife still hung out with her rich friends but her husband, me, was a deadbeat.

Still, *New York Magazine* named me the "41st Reason to Love New York." I was oddly eccentric. There was attention around me even though I didn't accomplish anything that was normal like earning money.

I visited my father in Florida once or twice a year. I used to play tennis and golf with him. My mom used to nag him a lot when she was alive and now that she was dead I think he found peace on the golf course. When he moved to Florida my wife let me move back in with her.

Dad loved my mother a lot when she was alive but found life a lot easier when she was gone. She had been particularly harsh on him when she was dying. He did his best but it was never good enough. She pinned a target on his back and kept throwing venomous darts at him.

Dad died in 2014. It hurt me badly. I used to walk down the streets of New York and see him when he wasn't there. I needed him as my dead companion. He was my paternal ghost. He had been the major influence in my life. I hated insurance. But he talked me into going into it. I made a lot of money and I still have dribs and drabs of that money that I use to get by today. Without my dad encouraging me into going into insurance I'd probably be homeless. Insurance bored me but saved me.

I am a writer. I always was a writer. I believe that I am a genius. If you disagree with me, you can drop dead.

I have a lot of published books, "The King of White Collar Boxing" (Rain Mountain Press,) "In Jail: The Essays" (Prison Federation), "Lane Changes "(Four Way Books), "Dementia Pugilistica," (Turtle Bay Press), "Blame it on the Scientists" (Pudding House Poetry Chapbook), and "Living On Madison Avenue," (Future Cycle Press). "In the Suburbs of Suicide" (Adelaide Publishing), a novel, was published in February 2020.

I also published a thousand poems in magazines and hundreds of political articles in *Daily Caller, American Thinker* and *Canadian Forum.* While I used to be a liberal socialist when I was a rich kid living in Great Neck, years down the line after jail I became a conservative. In college during the sixties I was also a progressive. It seems that spoiled Democrats don't have the courage to have moral values and to make distinctions. In jail I knew what was right and wrong. I was in a Federal Prison Camp but I wished I was in a penitentiary so that I would have to fight for my life. I believed in the death penalty. Part of me wished that the system would execute me. For tax evasion? Was I nuts?

I sleep in my son's bedroom. He is married and lives in Brooklyn. I like having my own room to myself as I previously liked living with my parents. As you get older and can taste your death like meat in a doggie bowl you begin to need a little space. This does not mean that I want separation.

When my wife kicked me out of her bedroom she said it was because I got up too many times during the night to piss. She was a light sleeper. I could care less if she woke every few hours to take a dump. But I didn't like the way she took up three quarters of the bed and left me hanging over the side. Sometimes she would have a bad dream and wake me to discuss it with me. She was the dream columnist for the *Daily News* and knew a lot about dreams. Sometimes when she woke me I felt like punching her. I never did that. I was not a wife beater. I was not Floyd Mayweather even if I was a half-ass boxer.

I knew that I didn't really want to hit her. My latest psychiatrist told me these were intrusive thoughts. I fantasized about things I had no desire to do. I wanted to punish myself.

She kicked me out of her room but I felt like she was doing me a favor. I was fifty years old back then and could take or leave sex. I just wanted enough space in bed so I was not caught up in her dreams.

When I die I hope I can come together again with my wife, hold hands and walk off into the heavens. She is all that I want out of life at this stage. We have been married over forty years and I feel like she is my limb. She is my wife and mother. She is my sister. She is part of me and the whole of me.

I wish I knew how important she would be to me when I was younger. She has become my orbit. I spin around with her.

If I make every minute we are together important we will be together for a million years.

In the future children with telescopes will look up at us and see that we are stars in the sky. We will be looking down at the earth and realize that we made the future beautiful.

I hope our son looks for us with the telescope of his heart. I hope both of our writings eclipse the superficial authors of our generation.

Leor Returns

Leor was an old boxing student of mine during 2008-2012. He came two to three times a week and sparred a lot but never competed in a tournament. At the time he was in his twenties and worked as a stock broker in a bucket shop.

He was making a good living but not great. He was flashy and had a rented Mercedes. He used to brag that he'd go to discos and buy four hundred-dollar bottles of booze. That didn't impress me. Even when I was a millionaire I didn't like to be taken advantage of by clubs. I was not a sucker. I didn't want to feel that I was being taken advantage of my sleezeballs.

Leor was a stocky, tough guy who looked like he wasn't the type to backdown from any confrontation. He was an Israeli. A person from a tiny country surrounded by millions of Arabs who wanted to wipe them off the face of the earth. I respected Israelis. They were tougher than New York Jews. They weren't liberals who felt sorry for their enemies.

When Leor used to train with me, I was in my late fifties. We used to spar quite a bit. He was stronger than me but I had been a pro and knew how to handle myself. Surprisingly, boxing is a sport of comradery. We used to hug each other after sparring and pat each other on the backs. Aggression sometimes leads to warm feelings of friendliness. It is the reverse of its intention. It is nice. We felt like brothers. We were proud of our courage and relished our bruises and blackeyes. For someone reason I felt affection in my aggression. It's kind of emotional to try to hurt each other. It's togetherness.

****

Not having spoken to Leor in years, I was delighted to hear from him when he called me and told me he wanted to make an appointment to box with me. Things were a little slow at Gleason's Gym now that the pseudo boxing gyms like *Equinox* and *Pedal and Punch* had opened around the corner.

So welcome aboard Leor. I could use the extra business and it would be good to pick up a few extra bucks and nice to see an old friend.

On July 6th, 2019 Leor showed up at Gleason's. He looked about the same age, although it was more than ten years later. I felt like I had seen him just yesterday.

I thought back to the times when I used to really spar with Leor. He was strong as a moose. He used to bench press three hundred pounds. He was less than half of my age.

I'd try to keep our sparring sessions nice back then. But sometimes I'd hear angry voices in my head and try to break his ribs. I broke a lot of guys ribs. I was the rib breaker. I'd get all my weight into my body shots. I turned my hip back and then sprung it forward, locking the hooking arm to my side.

One of the reasons that I was so good to the body now was because I made hitting to the head taboo. I had minor brain damage so we never hit to the head when we sparred. If Leor did hit me in the temple I'd probably become religious, stupid. I'd be a money changer on the temple steps and Leor would overturn all my coins. I tried not to hit him too hard in the head because he wasn't allowed to hit me in the head and that wouldn't have been fair.

However, one time I hit him with an uppercut that was as beautiful as the air around the Matterhorn. It was loose like snow and drifted into his chin like a Christy stop. It was light but hard like a swimmer punching the water.

Then I hit him in the ribs with a boomerang. He bent over and almost fell to the floor. I liked him but I hoped I broke his ribs. I wanted to feel powerful. *Men's Journal* once printed an article on me, "America's Oldest Professional Wants to Kill Someone."

Leor stopped. He was in a fair bunch of pain. I told him, "We're friends so it doesn't matter if you stop. But if you're in a real fight and your opponent sees you're hurt he'll get excited and kill you."

I didn't want Leor to stop. He was too tough for that. He had to hang in there if he was going to be a boxer.

Leor thanked me for the advice. I taught him something about boxing and something about courage. The rate at that time for a lesson was 25 dollars. He gave it to me.

He learned from me about skill and courage. I learned something from him, "I'm young,/ I'm alive./ I'm still a real/Motherfucker."
****

Well, the next time Leor was back in the gym we decided we wouldn't spar. I had him hit the heavy bags and we did the mitts. I usually like to spar everyday. But Leor was a bit heavy and strong for me.

He told me what happened to him in the last few years. He didn't go to jail like me but he lost his broker's license and he was working at his parents' falafel restaurant. I felt bad for him. He had an enormous ego and I couldn't imagine him being happy with a job at a restaurant. I remember that I heard from him a number of years ago when his brother died in a motorcycle accident. That was a tough blow. He loved his brother. Leor was a good family man.

When you haven't seen a person in years you get a feeling about him. I felt like Leor had fallen on bad times. If it were the old days and I still had money I might have helped him. But now I could hardly help myself and I had gone from the king of insurance to a boxing trainer. I had fallen into social mediocrity while I was still writing books and reaching up for the fountain pen in the sky.

Leor was just passing through. It was good to hitch-hike with him into our past. He looked the same. He wasn't. He was damaged. I shared failure crouching on the sidelines with him.

I wondered if he'd come back for another lesson. Could he afford it? I'd like to see him again. Who knows what he could afford or what he wanted to do with the rest of his life?

His life was trickling out from under him. Mine was dramatic. It included jail and professional boxing. Mine was what movies were made from. There were several options on my life story but they never came to anything. It's all there in my book, *The King of White-Collar Boxing.* It will probably never go anywhere either. Yet I feel like I can fly. I am character from *Peter Pan.*

The Invention of White Collar Boxing

This story was originally published in "Boxing Scene Magazine" in 1990. It is about how I invented white collar, businessman boxing which eventually became popular amongst thousands of businessmen boxers in numerous countries.

HOW I WON THE MOST EDUCATED FIGHT IN THE HISTORY OF PUGILISM

by David Lawrence

11:00 A.M.-February 15,1990

I am Superman. I eat Wonderbread. Smack my face. I am alive.

Tonight, I am scheduled to fight a 5-round smoker for Gleason's New York State White Collar Welterweight Championship. It's a club fight, unsanctioned by either the Amateur Boxing Federation or the New York Athletic Commission. I am 42. Both organizations feel I should be bowling. I feel like John Heenan, wearing disguises, sneaking around the London countryside to fight.

Tonight's fight promises to be the most educated battle in the history of pugilism. My opponent, Doc Richard Novick, has a law and a veternarian's degree. I have a Ph.D. in literature and am the President of Allied Programs Corporation, a Wall Street insurance brokerage firm. Grow up boys. Make us.

I remember the first time I saw the Doc.

12:30 P.M. - November 18, 1985

What am I doing in this place, Gleason's Gym? Pugs all over the place. Look at that wiry, white one, jumping the rope in between the black heavyweight and the short, stocky Hispanic.

His body is tight as a drum. His abdominals are like a mogul field. I wouldn't fight him for all the tea in China. That face, or better yet, that nose. I can't look at it -- it's an accident that has already happened. It turns around on itself like a snail. The shell is bifurcated and moves off in different directions. It's sick. Sickening. How could a person willingly misshape himself so? Yet, he must be proud of his nose. It is a trophy, a trumpet of his toughness. Otherwise, why not fix it?

His face is gone. Who would fight him? He has nothing to lose. I wouldn't. I'll never be like him. Never. Neverland. Promise, honor-bright, first star I see tonight. I'll never fight the Doc.

In and About 1985-1990
I begin to run into the Doc regularly at the gym. At this time he is sparring with the likes of Roberto Duran, Alexis Arguello, Billy Costello, Donnie Poole, Livingstone Bramble, etc. He's been at it about 20 years. He predates the age of the white collar boxers, which spawned me. He is the real thing. He has fought three professional fights to prove it. In between, he runs a highly successful vetinary practice. He is 44 years old on the night of the most educated fight.

7:00 A.M. -- July 12, 1987
I am sparring with the Doc. I never thought it would come to this point. Am I as crazy as the Doc if I step into the ring with him? If he hits me, do I become him?
I am still green around the ears, under the headgear. My trainer, Hector Roca, tells him to go easy on me. I giggle (nerves) and remind the Doc that I am only a beginner (chicken).

I tap him a few times on the nose. Can't miss it. It's a bud vase. A little purple flower grows.

He throws a long overhand right. It lands square on my temple. I wobble. The Cantor in my head blows the "shofar."

I smile. Get angry. Land a few rib-rattlers.

He tosses an uppercut. Very nonchalant. I can't eat for three days.

10:00 P.M.-January 13, 1990
Donnie Poole, the Canadian welterweight champ, is sparring with me. He is built like Popeye. I am Olive Oyl, limbs flying about the ring as I sumble about in retreat. I am a bird, with one foot caught in a fence, arms wildly flapping to get free.

Poole is a good guy. He takes it easy on me. We get out of the ring and bullshit. He tells me fighters want to get hurt. He is just learning how not to want to suffer. He is a philosopher. I am interested because we share certain views about boxing and life. He suggests I write his life story. I agree.

After I shower, Hector and Poole are standing outside Hector's office.
"Davey can beat the Doc," I hear Hector saying.

Poole bets $500 on the Doc's behalf.
"Davey bets $500 too," Hector says. "You kill the Doc, Davey," Hector adds.

The bet is made. Thus spoke Hector. If I backed out I'd lose face.

The date is set for two weeks later.

10:00 A.M.-January 20,1990
Gleason's Gym. The fight is rescheduled for February 15. Donnie says the Doc is giving his $500 to him if he wins. I offer my purse

to Hector. Now Hector has a stake in the fight. He won't let me lose. Even if he has to come out of the corner and hit Doc himself.

11:20 A.M.-February 15, 1990
It's a decadent, degenerate thing to do. Entirely, self-destructive. I love it. We'll see who destroys who.

But soft, anon, nuncle, I mustn't get too beat up.
The wife thinks I am at a business meeting. She doesn't suspect my adulterous "liason dangereuse" with a pair of boxing gloves. If my face is battered, should I say negotiations were rough? Or quip that we clashed heads for awhile, then saw eye to eye?

Defense. Defense. I must come home unblemished.

I am eager. I am nervous. I am scared shitless. Yet I am anonymously making history. Two fighters with their educational titles on the line. A freak show.

Is boxing a way out of the ghetto? I will rise above the tenements of my despair, the abandoned buildings of my confidence.

Why? Because Everlast is there. Because the Doc is there. Because I shouldn't be there. Because I was brought up nice. Because I will burn the niceties of my upbringing and rise above the ashes like a phoenix into a heavenly gutter of tenement toughness. I am Henry Higgins betting that I can turn My Fair Lady into Eliza Dolittle.

Will my mother be there? In spirit. She will hold the metal Enswell under my eye and go, "There, there, son. You shouldn't be hurting other people's hands with your dear, sweet head."

I am Salamo Arouch in Auswitz. All the Jews are burning. I am told I can live if I put on boxing exhibitions. I have been given a one-way ticket to freedom. The Boxing Commisssion can't see this. Boxing is my salvation. I don't want to die by fire.

7:00 P.M. - February 15, 1990

I check out the arena. No one is there. It's a surreal scene. Darkness except for a lone spotlight on the ring. I think of Rocky Balboa going into the gym late at night to have a private grudge match with Apollo Creed. Just to do it. To see who is the better man.

I've been driven udnerground into this private, unsanctioned world. There won't even be an attending physician. Doctors, heal thyselves. I am in the Twilight Zone, beating out the dilemma of my own competetiveness on the anvil of this bout. I am high society gone back to its roots in the mean streets.

I was born an aesthetic. I am an intellectual. But we are in America. The mind here has commercial value. You might as well hit yourself in the head and sell tickets to the fight. I will.

7:15 P.M. - February 15, 1990
I am in Bruce Silverglade's private office in Gleason's. Doc Novick arrives. How have you been? Long time no see.

Doc has prepared waivers of liability. He sure must be confident. But I'd never sue. He is losing the poetry of the moment in legal concerns. He is not concentrating on the fight. This fight is above the law. It is illegal in the first place. Waivers are candyass. Let's get it on.

Richard, I'm surprised. We are here to die and you are worried about the law. There are greater laws than what you studied in your books. The laws of nature. Thousands of years of civilization and

we are still animals. Why else are we fighting, Richard? You're becoming too civilized. Perhaps, you are vulnerable.
Yet look at your nose. Surely, that is uncivilized. Or is the obsessiveness of the civilized man. Your task is to build the ugliest nose. You have lost all perspective. You are a weightlifter with 25" biceps. You are Bottom in *Midsummer's Night Dream*, in love with an ass. You are Alec Guiness in *Bridge over the River Kwai*. You are in love with your own nose. Your goal is nasal annihilation. You follow it like an automaton. You are no longer part of nature. You are a soldier. I will devour you. I am a cat.

Looking back, I'm not sure how the fight actually came about.

8:00 P.M. - February 15, 1990

The ring. The Doc and I wish each other luck. Bruce Silverglade places two huge trophies in the ring. He announces that this is the beginning of a series of white collar tournaments, which he hopes will grow into an international event. We are fighting for the vacant, welterweight crown.
The bells ring. I am calm. The world is in slow motion. I am in the zone. Every punch I throw lands. His face is swelling up like a pink waterballoon. I double jab him. A straight right sneaks in and knocks him back 15 feet into the ropes. The ref, Johnny Rivera, former contender for the middleweight crown, gives the Doc a standing eight-count. I don't finish him off because I'm worried about conserving energy for the five rounds.

I am back in my corner. Hector is too drunk to stand on the apron, so he directs me from the side. Chino tells me to uppercut and hook. Hector tells me if I keep doing good he'll get me my pro license.

In Round Two, the Doc becomes a human punching bag. I hit him. His head snaps back, then foward. He has no defense. His nose is onion purple. I think he likes it.

Round three exhausts both of us. Donnie Poole keeps yelling he's got me. Which fight is he watching?

Between rounds, Hector tells me to go easy and save it for the fifth. I dance. I am Baryshnikov with heavy legs. Baryshnikov is playing Gregor in Metamorphosis. I am a cockroach. Fast and indestructible. I don't get hurt.

Round Five. I am smoking. I am Fred Astaire, tapdancing on his face. He knows he has to stop me. He throws bombs. But I catch them and throw them back. He likes being blown up. He never quits. He fights till the last bell.

The victory is mine. It is sweet. The 20 or so people there applaud. The scorecard reads 10-8, 10-9, 10-10, 10-9. No contest.

I can't believe how easily I mastered the same fellow who scared the shit out of me a few years before. Did he get worse? Did I improve? Does six days a week of practice really help?

8:30 P.M. - February 15, 1990

The screwing. I'm upstairs in the dressing room. Ecstatic. Novick comes in to congratulate me. We hug. Pals to the end. He splits.

Poole enters and says, "Doc's trying to stiff you out of the $500. Come down with me and tell him to pay."

"I don't want to fight over the money," I answer.

Poole grabs Hector to help him.

I have already given Hector $200 to pay the officials. I was supposed to be winning money, not losing it. After all, I did win the fight.

Poole is back. "The motherfucker won't pay. He's a disgrace. I thought he could fight. He's only good for sparring. Dave, lend me th $500 so I can pay Hector."
"It makes me look like a jerk. And he's not even coming to dinner. He was supposed to treat all of us. He's the worst sport I ever knew. I'll break his fuckin' neck. He's embarrassed cause he thought you wre nothing, but you're a better man than he is. He's a faggot."

Hector returns.

"Don't worry kid. I'll take care of you," I say.

"Forget it. You won. That's all that counts," Hector answers.

9:00 A.M.-February 16, 1990

The morning after. The office. The Doc is on the phone. "I'm calling about dinner. Let's go out. The $500, though, I knew nothing about. Poole made that bet on his own."

"It was Hector's money, Doc. It doesn't matter to me personally, but he could use it," I say.

"But the bet wasn't mine. Poole set up the whole thing. Even the fight," he said. "You wanted to turn pro and Randy Gordon said if you beat me it would be okay.

I didn't want to fight. I didn't even know till I got there that you had had 13 amateur fights. I figured you were like the old days, when I could take you easy."
"I didn't challenge you. Poole said you wanted to fight me. And this fight had nothing to do with turning pro," I said.

"Then Poole fucked us."

"Forget about it, Doc. The money's not that important."

9:20 A.M. - February 16, 1990

I get an urgent call from Poole. "That cheap son of a bitch," he says. "I'll break his fuckin' neck. I thought he was a friend but he's just a faggot. He's just not paying because he's so embarrassed he lost."

"Forget about it, Poole. I'm sure there was just a miscommunication. Let's all try to stay friends."

"He shouldn't have done that to me."

"It's me who got stuck for the money."

But the money wasn't the issue. All I cared about was winning the fight. I am now Gleason's New York State White Collar Welterweight Champion. My title is open to anyone who wants to take it way.

Next time I don't think I'll bet on the results. Win or lose, it ends up too expensive.

Boxer Rebellion

I made a documentary about my boxing life from 1991-1994. I wrote it, starred in it and produced it. It cost me about three hundred and fifty thousand dollars at the time when I was under examination by the Feds and my business was going downhill. I was desparate. I needed a hit. So I let the money fly.

Celia, the director, whom my wife hated, told me that the film, *Boxer Rebellion,* made it into the Sundance Film Festival. My wife accused me of bribing the officials. She had not seen the movie but she was convinced that it stank. Maybe she was right. Or maybe it was too good to be entertaining. Maybe it was too deep and the movie forgot to laugh at itself. In any event it was not superficial. It was not surface. It was deep and artistic. Oh well, It might have been boring and messy.

If anything, me and my crew were serious about *Boxer Rebellion.* Celia was part of the Warhol crowd. She was a friend of my oldest friend Kenny and he was the one that recommended that she should make a documentary about me.

I remember when I met Celia at Warhol's factory. She seemed arty enough to startle the middle-class world. I wanted to be different. Actually, I was.

The cameraman, Jean Marie Meyer, was Celia's husband. Sundance was the big kahuna. It was like the Cannes Film Festival. My bipolar ego went wild and I thought that I was going to become a skinny Orson Welles even though I was the producer not the director. I liked film even though I didn't respect the process of piecing a movie together. It was too mechanical and involved a crew rather than one's examining one's individual psyche. I was a poet. I liked to be conquered by words. Movies were made by technicians for dummies. I didn't like crews. I wanted to dive into my own psyche.

Sundance Film Festival was held at Park City Utah, which was a good ski area that I skied at with my son and my dad. When we wanted to go really posh we'd go down the road to Deer Valley. They restricted the ski sales to five thousand people a day. They had tissue boxes on the trees on the lift lines. You put your skiis on in a hut attached to the lodge.

Once we sat next to billionaire Carl Icahn at the Deer Valley Lodge. He was amazed when my five-year-old son ordered caviar. It was one of the rare times I saw him laughing. He was too rich to smile.

When we had a screening of *Boxer Rebellion* in New York at Du Arts my wife refused to come. She had good reason. She had had a fight with Celia and Celia had thrown a piece of sushi at her at a Japanese Restaurant. I should have backed my wife but I was afraid that Celia would drop out of the movie about me and I would lose my shot at fame while I was in the process of losing my business.

A few weeks later I went to jail. Celia wrote to me from Sundance that we were a big hit. We weren't. I asked the warden if I could get a furlough to go to Sundance. He didn't like movies. He didn't like me. He didn't think my entreaty to go to the festival was worth a reply. I had to be kidding. Of course, I didn't get to see it. Like all wardens he didn't have a sense of humor. When my roommate, Billy, hung himself the warden told me the news like he was reading off a menu. I don't know if he felt anything. I didn't care.

Later Emanuel Levy of *Variety* reviewed the film: *Drowned in striking visuals and dizzying sounds, but devoid of much substance , "Boxer Rebellion" is an impressionistic documentary about a Wall Street yuppie who became a professional boxer in middle age.... David Lawrence, a wealthy and powerful stockbroker, was quite content with his life until he discovered the allure, risk and challenge of the boxing world. At 44, Lawrence was not young, but with the assistance of a great trainer...he mastered the necessary skills and even excelled at the brutal sport..... Indeed, after 30 minutes or so, the surreal imagery and distorted sounds become so repetitious, and the disjointed symbols and metaphors pile up so voluminously, that it's understandable that "Boxer Rebellion" had the largest number of walkouts of any documentary shown this year at Sundance.*

Wow. I hadn't seen the Variety review in years. *The largest number of walkouts*? Was I a failure or was I so good that the idiots couldn't stay in their seats?

I guess I stank. And I was naïve enough to think that my movie would make me famous. I also was naïve enough to think that my three rap albums would make me rich. Or "Magic Man" which I wrote with Nina Simone's brother—Sam Waymon would make me a fortune. It got great reviews but I forgot to collect my money from Sam. I was negligent.

I was a brilliant colossal failure. I often wondered why my wife allowed me to move back into her apartment. Was it because I made her giggle?

But I was trying to write books and become an important writer. I was dead serious. I wanted to become something again. I wanted her to be comfortable with me like a pillow she lay her head down on. I published *The King of White Collar Boxing, On Jail: The Essays, Lane Changes and Living on Madison Avenue.*
I also published *Lane Changes and Dementia Pugilistica.* I had a few other books in the pipeline. Another book of poems—*Living on Madison Avenue* and a novel, *In the Suburb of Possible Suicide.* A contract on a poetry book in the U.K.—*Broken Paragraphs.*

I published a thousand poems in good magazines. I even published hundreds of conservative articles in *Daily Caller* and *American Thinker*.

I was written about in almost every newspaper and magazine including *People Mag., Men's Journal, Time Out, New York Magazine, The Wall Street Journal, The Post,The New YorkTimes,* etc. etc.

I earned my meager money teaching boxing at Gleason's Gym. I found I enjoyed my variegated life. I was glad that I didn't have to sell people insurance anymore. Frankly, I didn't care if the clients were covered or not and if their houses burned down and they couldn't collect. I am not the hall monitor. I don't help people to cross the street. I am a poet. I am the absence of details. I am a seagull. I fly. I am beyond the horizon when I am not on my lithium.

Iron Will Power

When I look back at the seventy-two years of my life I realize that I have extraordinary will power, iron will power. Every time I have made a decision I have stuck to it until the end. It was my iron will power that allowed me to straighten out my life.

****

I dabbled with drugs in the early sixties before the Beatles and the hippies had made them fashionable. I smoked marijuana before my high school mates had heard of it. I was ahead of the trends. There was a song, "I'm in with the in crowd" in 1964. I was seventeen. I was the *in crowd.* It was performed by Dobie Gray. Who cares? He isn't even a memory now. And the *in crowd* has become typically the out crowd, the corpse of previous enthusiasm.

****

One day in the sixties I told my mother that I was thinking of killing myself. I meant it only a little. But she panicked and sent me to a psychiatrist. Within a few sessions I stopped beating myself up, stealing my dad's Jaguar at night going one hundred and thirty miles per hour, taking her diet drugs and sleeping pills and getting into street fights. I didn't know that I had such willpower but I did. I became a new person. I realized that I was not what I seemed but that what I wanted to be. I couldn't even relate to the old sloppy degenerate who I had been. I found meaning in being other than who I was. I celebrated life not self-destruction. I willed my willpower to steel. I became a nerd and respected it. I no longer wanted to be cool.

****

When my older brother told me that my thighs were chunky, like tree trunks, my will power kicked in again and I started a weight lifting program and went on a low calorie diet. I weighed only 160 pounds but I felt it was too much. My will power kicked in and I added diet to my exercise. I ate salads and cans of tuna. I stopped all starches, cakes, candies and non-diet sodas. I never finished a portion and always left some on the table. I dropped to 135 pounds during the summer.

I am now 72 years old and weigh 142 pounds. In my forties I boxed pro as a 147 pound welterweight. I wanted to get down to junior welterweight but I couldn't. I would have been more formidable. I have always watched my weight since my brother commented about my thighs.
****
At the end of eleventh grade at Great Neck North HighSchool I found my will power with regard to studying. I had been getting all C's and wasn't even aware of it. I didn't consider that I would have no future with such bad grades. I didn't even realize that what I was doing was wrong. It never even occurred to me to study.

I remember running into Jimmy Cogell. He was a good student and a good athlete. He was part of the upwardly mobile snobs. I remember his saying, "You're not as stupid a everyone thinks." I suddenly realized that I was presenting myself to everyone as a dummy. I was cutting school, fighting, drugging, drinking and just not giving a damn. I didn't want to be other people's bad image of me. Once again I put my iron will power into high gear, dropped all my bad-influence friends and started studying. I came straight home from school and sat at my desk. I wouldn't even answer my phone. I realized that other students were just distractions.

It was ironic that my parents had moved me to Great Neck to inspire me to study. Instead it just made me fail worse. I realized that good grades were unrelated to the school but contingent on my will power in studying.

When I forced myself to study furiously, I conquered my negative tendencies and became a straight A student all the way through until my Ph.D.

It was not that I was stupid. I was lazy. I was always intelligent. I didn't realize that application was accomplishment. That I could make myself a good student but that a good school could not turn me into a valedictorian.

I always laugh at politicians who want to make the schools better rather than to improve the students. You don't take the student out of the school. You take the student out of himself and his bad habits.

****

Another example of my tremendous will power was when I quit cocaine. I had had about a two year habit. Everyone in the eighties was doing it. I was in the insurance business and everytime I walked into a broker's office he offered me a couple of lines. I had such a bad habit that I used to snort before going to sleep. I used vodka to calm me down.

One day I walked into my apartment and noticed that there wasn't much furniture. It occurred to me that I was spending a lot of what I earned on cocaine and that if I really wanted to furnish my apartment well I'd have to cut back on the coke. If you've ever kicked drugs, you'd realize what will power you need to do it.

I pulled a little trick. Two big mafiosa types came up to my office in the Kodak Building at 43rd Street and Sixth Avenue. I gave them two grand and they went on their merry way and left me a manilla envelope of coke.

Then I repeated my youthful trick where I practiced portion control on food to get my thighs thinner. I took the two thousand dollars worth of coke down to the bathroom and controlled my intake by flushing it down the toilet. And I promised myelf that I would continue to punish myself by flushing my money down the toilet. I felt relieved. I didn't want any more coke because it cost me too much for nothing. I was spending thousands on the toilet. My will power was iron.

The next week I bought five hundred dollars worth of coke. The same muscle men delivered it to my office. When they left I walked down to the bathroom and flushed it away. Never again in all these years did I snort cocaine. I had taught myself a lesson by throwing out my coke. It temporarily hurt my wallet. I didn't want to hurt myself again so I never purchased coke again.
****
When I went to jail in 1993 I realized that I had failed somewhere in life. It was only tax evasion but I had to have fallen pretty low to end up in Schuylkill Federal Prison Camp.

I was obviously not gay so there was no chance of my having sex in jail. But when I walked in I swore I would never flirt with another woman except my wife. I felt that I should be true to my relationship and that I should be an honest, upright citizen.

When I watched my dorm mates looking at sleezy magazines such as *Hustler Magazine* I was sickened by the human body. I told myself I wanted to make love to my wife not to masturbate to some photo of a woman I didn't even know. When I jerked off in the shower I thought only of my wife. I was masturbatory monogamous. I wanted a human not a sexual relationship.

Interestingly when I came out of jail in 1995 I still only fantasized about sex with my wife. I never touched another woman and that was kind of rare for my generation. Sex like crime had become something rather disgusting to me. I was not looking to lose myself in sexual numbness but to find myself in my intellect, *ad hoc* poems and my relationship with my wife.

I pretty much gave up fantasizing about sex as I had given up almost everything else.

****

The last thing I gave up was neurological drugs. I had had some brain injuries from my previous boxing bouts. I had been seeing Dr. Charney who had been treating me, mostly for failed short term memory.

I went through a series of drugs—Memantine, Donepezil, Acetazolamide and Gabapentin. Maybe there were some other drugs too.

My problem with all of these drugs was that they made me sleepy, forced me to bend over with poor posture and gave me leg cramps. I also lost about ten pounds and looked rail skinny. Instead of clearing up my thoughts these pharmaceutical drugs confused me.

One day in May of 2019 Dr. Charney told me to stop all my drugs and see how I reacted. Once again this required iron will. But I did it anyway and much to my surprise within a few days I felt much livelier, put on weight, improved my posture and got rid of the leg cramps.

****

I am proud of how my iron will came forward to save me. I was kept from going astray by my ability to cut short my failed behavior. What separated me from a drug addict or a divorcee was my iron will. I had self-control. I would only let myself tickle the notes of going astray. I would not self-destruct. I would not play a concert of failure. I would not fall off the keyboard.

Tough Stuff

Kelly's friend, Nick, delivered fifty thousand dollars in hundred dollar bills to my office in a brown bag. Kelly had been laundering the money through Nick. At the time I didn't know that Nick was gay and that Kelly was gay. I suppose that made me the head of a gay money laundering ring. Being homophobic, that didn't sit too well with me. I liked women. They could be annoying but they were sexual creatures who intrigued me as if they flew down in flying saucers to capture me. As for men, I got along with them but they sexually nauseated me. I just wasn't into them. They were companions to do sports with or to boast with about our female conquests.

Kelly was as fake as counterfeit money. He was married with three children and pretended that he was the family man of the year. He bragged about the number of women he supposedly hit on. In the meantime he owned a gay escort service and was in love with his lead male prostitute. He was paying for his hormone shots to become a woman. I don't know why he wanted to help his boyfriend become a woman when he wasn't attracted to women. I guess his boyfriend was a whiner. He must have insisted. I didn't know this until we were all indicted for money laundering. Then the feds spilled the beans on him.

Kelly and I divided up the piles of hundred dollar bills. I decided to take a walk down at the seaport just to dare the authorities to grab my money which I had put in a Louis Vitton briefcase. I liked money. My briefcase cost a thousand dollars. I was spoiled.

I felt rich passing along the East river on my way to the Seaport. I imagined someone attacking me and trying to steal my briefcase. I would have killed him. I would have thrown him on the ground and kicked him in the head until he was dead. I kicked friends in the head when I was a teenager. Some friend? I don't think I could have become a hit man. Maybe a kick man.

As I was walking along I bumped into the king of crime, himself, John Gotti. He was walking along with a body guard past Sloppy Louis. It wasn't Sammy the Bull. I knew Sammy from Gleason's Gym where he used to spar with Adolfo Viruet. Of course, Viruet wouldn't hit him too hard. He had never killed a man. Sammy had murdered at least nineteen men. I couldn't help but feel that I could out box Sammy the Bull. He was a tough guy who out-toughed other men with a knife or a gun. He was a mean rooster, a cock with claws. But he was never much of a boxer.

So my chauffeur became friendly with Sammy's driver. I sort of got a kick about their going out to dinner together. I felt like I was mafia, connected by my driver.

I was shocked to run into Gotti who was wearing a trench coat like Humphry Bogart in *Casablanca.* I was disgusted and impressed. This was before I had been to jail. I kind of looked up to him. He was shorter than me but he made men fearful.

He was carrying a Guicci briefcase. It occurred to me that I might be carrying more hundred dollar bills than he was. That made me feel big. I was richer than John Gotti. Maybe I was the real gangster. Maybe I existed as something other than an insurance broker. I wanted to pat myself on the back but I was afraid that he would think that I was reaching for a gun.

Gotti didn't look so tough to me. I wanted to say, "John, I'm the man." Did I have to compete with everyone. And why would I want to give a psychopath the initiative to be psychopathic?

Running into Gotti gave me a lift. But he took advantage of people and I was a schmuck. I had endorsed Kelly's stealing from me and

I was more of a sucker than a criminal. I would go to jail for someone else's crime. I was robbing from myself. I was laundering my own money when there was no reason to turn it into cash. I could have just written myself a check for it.

I was a sort of gratuitious criminal. I was not sweaty palmed and needing money. I could burn money. It was just fun and games to me. I wasn't desperate. I was more *noblesse oblige.*

When I got out of jail I gave boxing lessons to Carmine Persico's nephew. Nice kid. He looked like a little librarian. It's funny the way people turn out different from what they seem. It's stupid the way I never looked beneath the surface for the real person lumbering beneath the waves.

Kelly ruined my life. But I was swift enough to find it in the backyard amongst the leaves and set fall fires to my celebration, to find another way to live without regrets. I didn't know what I was doing but I did it anyway. I became a felon when I was as innocent and naïve as a lamb.

Essays In And Around Tough Love

Forget White Supremacy

The left wing flies. Our country dies. We were not meant to be communists or revolt against our values. America's greatness is embedded in its capitalism. Communism has never worked and despite it's myth of sharing has always become totalitarianism. Communism and fascism are the same. They are just different coats on borrowed bodies.

There is no white supremacy. If a group does better than another it is part of temporary history. There are just people doing their best for hundreds of years. Tradition is tradition. It could have been whites, blacks, yellows or reds who were supreme first.

Supremacy is the name losers label those who have become superior to them. Competition could erase the label.

White supremacy is not prejudice. It's the luck of the draw in a borrowed casino. It's a position not an ambition. It's where a race has arrived at due to hard work and luck.

So many whites complaining about white supremacy. They hate themselves for their accomplishments. Don't they look in the mirror and see that they are white. They imagine they are generous in cursing themselves out. Suicide is not giving to the wind. Blacks forgive whites their success. They want to imitate it. They are not jealous of whites. They want to be them. And they are becoming them.

Blacks have done so well since I was a boy in the fifties. Their own greatness and development should be celebrated not diminished. But the whites regard the blacks as failures and blame themselves because they hate themselves.

Complaints backfire against themselves. I am sick of Sharpton's sad, bitter, barking dog-face complaining in a country that has been too good for a tax-evader, riot engendering weight-shifter.

Sharpton does not encourage blacks to be the best they can be. He tells them to be angry and to protest rather than to meld with America's community. He doesn't understand that hatred breeds failure.

Progressives accuse Trump of saying bad things and condemn him to the ninth circle of words. Dante's in hell. He created his own final solution and laughed at himself in a divine comedy.

You call our President a racist for the black folderol of his sayings and the way he eats his own words. They are chewy. They are delicious. They are free speech unlike the left's rigid hatred and the Democrats' spiteful judgments. Unlike progressive regression.

If you always go left you will never be right. Left is revolution. It throws the world out of joint and promotes needless confusion and deaths. Conservative tradition is what holds the world in orbit.

Words are words. They do not kill unless they are misinterpreted by maniacs. Sincere liberals take words too seriously. They talk but don't act. They are all chatter and mumbo jumbo.

You give Trump no credit for improving the army and raising the living standards of the blacks and Hispanics. You stick Obama's food stamps on your forehead. You should mail yourself to political dissolution and hurtful revolution.

You are you who is a hand pulling the rug out from our President's feet. You have no soul. You are an attachment to the clichés of resentment.

You do not realize that other countries are laughing about your own rebellion against our government. Your criticisms makes us weak and embarrasses us.

The good you think you do is the bad that muddies our image to the world.
Trump is who he is, not the failed words of those who want to pull him out of the tree of his tall orders. Back in 1991 I shared a dressing room with Larry Holmes at the Taj Mahal. Donald Trump came in to see Holmes and ignored me.

In my book "The King of White Collar Boxing I said Trump "was the supreme egotist. Worse than me." But that wasn't true. I was just hurt because he paid more attention to Larry Holmes than to me. Who wouldn't? I was no one. Holmes was a great chamption. But that was before Trump took charge of our country and pulled us out of the weak effeminate hands of Obama.

So many people hate Trump. Their hatred reflects on their self-evaluations and their failure to celebrate Trump's successes.

I knew at the beginning that Trump was better than all the poseur Democrats when he demolished the Syrians who had bombed a school with chemical weapons. He stood up for what he stood up for when Obama was kneeling before Arab leaders.
When Obama made a friendly speech to all the Muslims in Cairo I knew that the Jews had voted for the wrong man. I am the Renegade Jew. You know, that guy on You Tube. I am not a good Jew. But I am better than those liberal Jews who backed their enemy—Obama. I do not go to temple. I am a temple of values. And now my brother Jews hate Trump who has been the greatest supporter

of Israel in history. He brought Jerusalem back as the capital. He has let the world know that we have Israel's back.

It's automatic that the liberals are negative when it comes to our president. Are they that stupid or are they just looking for a way to worm back into power and return the Democrats to the throne?

Trump is a bump on the road to greatness. He is an interference who actually becomes a positive reinforcement of free speech and Democracy.

Imagine discounting all Trump's good work because liberals don't like his tweets. They find truth awkward. They confuse Trump's clumsiness with their failure to improve America. They are so dumb that if they put their thumbs in a pie they would break the crust of our country's greatness.

Americans are judgmental. They break into factions and hate each other. Two new mass killings in El Paso and Dayton. And the angry children want to blame Trump instead of looking into their souls and recognizing that Americans have something wrong in their hearts and their heads.

We are bad. Do not point at our neighbors and try to pass the blame. We are blame. We are evil. And only in recognizing it can we begin to build a new world.

Fools blame mass murders on white supremacy. Did they stop to think that there are more mass murders by whites because there are more whites in this country? Did they stop to think that there are more black murders in Chicago because there are more blacks?

Perhaps whites commit more mass murders because they feel that they are part of the majority and can get away with it. Perhaps blacks are worried that they are in the minority and therefore kill on the individual level.

Martin Luther King, Jr. said that he wanted his children to “not be judged by the color of their skin, but by the content of their character."

There is no supremacy in color. There is only what you do or don’t do with it. Jealousy or anger are not accomplishments.

It seems that whites hate their own fictitious supremacy. Blacks accept white supremacy as a temporary situation and look forward to sharing in it. Whites hate themselves. Blacks want to share their good fortune.

In and Around Mass Killings

If I say bad things it is to cleanse my system of shards of negativity and to howl to the moon that I am not a dog but a paw sliding on a wet linoleum floor. I trip. I flip. I am the soft texture of a pancake and the nodule of a caper. I am in the air. I am manic. I am obsessed with one person and he is me. He, he. I laugh at my compulsions. When my wife called my warden in jail in 1994 and told him that I was bipolar, I thought she was crazy. I don't care. Labels are a form of adhesive tape. I was not a mass killer. I was a confused thinker.

I would never hurt an innocent victim because I don't believe in doing what I do when I don't and find solace in a backyard barbecue with my family still alive. America is a smorgasbord of mass killings. The map is littered with accidental, intentional corpses from El Paso to Dayton—two most recent killing fields.

And then the other dead *hors d'oeuvres*—Las Vegas, Orlando, Virginia Tech., Sandy Hook and on and on -- bodies falling off the earth. I once went to a Swedish restaurant with my father for lunch. I liked the tidbits and the fish. My dad is now dead. He was executed by God. Every hundred years or so the whole world is executed by God. It's funny that liberals don't believe in the death penalty when God specializes in it.

God is a bully, the biggest killer. I imagine him sitting up there in the clouds with an AK47. He doesn't care. He smokes a cigar. We all must go.

It's not that God is trying to depopulate the world so that we have more room for our expanding population. He doesn't care. How many centuries must it take for mankind to become aware that indifference has become God's form of love? Do you really think he cares if we are or aren't overpopulated?

Maybe God gets a kick out of killing us. Maybe he is a sadist. I doubt it. But what do I know? I don't know where I come from or where I am going. When I ride the subway, I don't know if I am going north or south. I am mysterious as the killer pieces in *Clue.*

I don't think God loves me. I don't think he loves or hates. He is the mirror that I look into to find my reflection. I spray paint on my face. I am hiding. I am going nowhere in a long-distance race called "life."

I am not an atheist. I hate atheist's as God deniers. They disrespect God. I respect him as the greatest mass murderer. I am afraid of him. But I don't know who he really is because I don't know who I am. He threw me onto the earth with a string attached to my ankle and I am bouncing on my head. I like the ride. I am glad that he put me here to suffer with a smile on my face.

I hate liberals who pretend that they are generous spirits and bend over backwards to offer nothing to the real killers. They are afraid to face God's destructiveness. They pretend that they feed the poor when they steal lambchops from the rich and pass them along to their self-created homeless.

Liberals shake my hand in a gesture of friendliness and then pull my fingers off and bury them in a punch bowl. Gee it's Halloween. They go dunking for fingernails. The strangle themselves and they drown.

You are a Democrat. You are an inhuman humanist and spread liberal kindness like poison jam on metal pieces of toast. Do you think anybody cares when you say you are not a racist and belittle your own race to feign allegiance to the minorities that you hate? You came out of the south and the Ku Klux Klan. You pretend that you are something when you are other. All your nice words to ethnic minorities don't give them roofs over their heads.

You pretend that you want to feed the poor and offer them pieces of glass so that they can not speak to you without bleeding on the air. You give the beggars a crust of bread while you live in a cake factory.

You call abortion women's health when you murder the female's child and leave health as an afterthought from a previous generation.

I know childbirth is an inconvenience but couldn't you give birth a chance. John Lennon wanted to give peace a chance. He is dead. So are millions of embryos. Liberals are made in God's image. That's why they kill. Sometimes in mass. Like God. Sometimes to our horror.

A Critique of Marianne Williamson's "A Return to Love" --Fifteen Years After

I am mildly reading Marianne Williamson's "A Return to Love." I am not looking to be one of her acolytes. I didn't really know she existed until I saw her babbling on the television about running for President. I am trying to find her faults so that I can ratify my rights, my intelligent conclusions, my understanding of what I understand as counterpoised to her religious, incestuous, less-than-bright ideas.

I am not going to read too muchof her book. Maybe just the introduction. I don't like to read anymore. I am seventy-two and don't have too many years to be who I am so I must write instead of read. I don't need to glean knowledge. I am knowledge.

Williamson is sweet but absorbedly stupid. Here's a simple-minded paragraph for me and you— "We were **taught to think** thoughts like competition, struggle, sickness, finite resources, limitation, guilt, bad, death, scarcity, and loss."

I don't think we were taught anything. I am the teacher not the student. My thoughts think themselves.
I am an atheist but I am more Godly than Williamson. We are what we are in the genetic insistence of our nervous systems. We are "death." We are what we are and not what we be. We accept "loss."

And where is love in all these horrors? Love is a fiction. It is a feeling that we feel towards others but can't define. Williamson says, "We came here to co-create with God by extending love."

Who's God? How does she have personal knowledge. I dare say if God wanted to make himself manifest he would appear to me before he'd bear witness to her. But God hides from me. He wants me to guess at his being. He would consider me stupid if I said I have personal knowledge of Him.

She goes on and on—"Love isn't material. It's energy." She is in the land of definitions. Love is the door that she opens to false meanings. In essence love is self-defined. It is what it is. It stands aside in an aisle in a theatre. It eats popcorn and drinks soda. It is full of itself.

Williamson defines fear as anger. She counterpoises this with love. But they are both the same. They are emotional turbulence in the gut. They are other than normal reality. They are heightened jests. Fear and love feel a little different but they are chemical congruents.

Williamson is alright for a skateboard without wheels. She frictions her way down the hill. She tries to make meaning out of meaning but buries declaration in failed outcomes. She shouldn't be a subject for me but I am attracted by her mediocrity and her pedestrian observation.

God bless her for trying. She is an ant hole looking at tininess through binoculars and seeing nothing but her own prejudices.

Vengeance and the Death Penalty

I don't believe in God but I believe in vengeance. The Bible says "Vengeance is mine; I will repay, saith the Lord." I agree but vengeances is not God's. God has nothing to do with vengeance. It is mankind's. It is our predilection. It is our right.

If God intercedes for us in vengeance he is coopting our responsibility. I would shake God by his crown for usurping my right to revenge. I don't need God to take my responsibility to get back at those I should get back at.

Retribution is evolution. It is the evolving of morality until where it gets its just deserts. It is man's responsibility.

I am vengeance. In order to get things right I have to get back at my enemies. If I free them from retribution than they will go on to commit other crimes or other criminals will feel they too can commit their crimes because there is no retaliation. A crime can only come close to being expunged by murdering the criminal. Death is the just result of the killer.

Lack of retribution is not heaven but is hell. Liberal morality is saying that we will let monsters free from their cages because we want to be generous as zoo keepers. But animals don't bear responsibility. Murderers know what they are doing when they kill innocents.

God wants vengeance but naïve people want to turn the other cheek. Thus they expose both cheeks to scars. A person who does not want vengeance betrays the beauty of retaliation and yanks down the scales of justice. The world become unbalanced. Civilization becomes unhinged. Even an absent God would want more fairness.

Torture is beautiful. Not to witness but to round out the symmetry of a ball room gown. Torture balances on glass slippers. It is a punishment that makes sense in getting back at the criminal's deed. Death is Cinderella. If a man rapes three women in a house and cuts them up with a machete, what fool wouldn't feel that the man does not only deserve the death penalty but that he should also be raped and tortured?

Vengeance means tit for tat. The killer rapist does not deserve a break when he has committed such heinous deeds. Letting him off the hook by putting him in jail for life vitiates the power of his nastiness. It redefines his heinous deeds as misdemeanors deserving amelioration rather than execution. By avoiding the death penalty his crime becomes insignificant. The grammar of the world becomes broken. Vengeance has its own alphabet.

Every killer on death row wants to get his sentence converted to life. Why should murderers get breaks? They have earned death. They deserve death. Death and torture. The liberals who believe that life in prison is a worse fate than death should see all the people on deathrow petitioning for life. I did a measly two years in jail. I liked it. I worked out. I read and I wrote. I made friends. I had no responsibilities. The food stank. Otherwise it was a celebratory experience.

God does not deserve the power of vengeance. Vengeance is ours. We are part of mankind. Our brothers and sisters have been killed. It is our responsibility to execute our killers. Cruelty is letting killers go without adequate punishment. God would not allowjustice to be so lopsided.

God is a cartoon. He has no right to kill. He is often the joke of goodness. We should never forgive. We should enter all the Death Rows and sweep out the killers with machine guns.

In fake liberalism where the person wants to believe that he is a good human being, you worry that we would kill an innocent man.

Liberals worry that we will execute the wrong people if we have the death penalty. They don't seem to care that the criminals almost always execute innocent people. If mass murderers kill innocence why can't we?

Ours is retribution not felonious assault. Vengeance is ours. We are the death of guilty killers. We keep the world and the scales of justice on balance.

We must have the courage of retribution. We must be strong enough to risk being wrong. The murderer kills helter skelter without worrying that he has killed the wrong victim. And the average killer spends twenty years on death row until he is executed. The average victim in the street gets a few minutes before he is killed. Fair is foul. The killer gets all the breaks

03519-015

Most of my friends know that I went to Schuylill Federsal Prison Camp in 1993. Many of them know that in my own contrarian way I liked it. I brag about it. I feel that I did something different from my business peers. I led a life outside the insurance realm.

The only way I could not be beaten by the prison system was to turn it around and make it fun. I was unlike those who were afraid of it and hated it. I became a cheerleader for the penal system. People who felt sorry for prisoners made me sick. I felt sorry for businessmen who had to price out policies and balance the boring books. I no longer had to go to boring lunches and dinners with dull brokers.

The food in prison was the worst in the world. Ours were returns from Desert Storm. They shipped them back from the dead soldiers.

The other prisoners complained about the food. What did they know? I was used to a charge account at Le Cirque and yet I never complained about the food. The slugs sitting next to me in the cafeteria didn't know Lutece from MacDonald's.
The number the feds gave me was 03519-015. But I was more than my number. I was David, the felon. I was cool. I wasn't an insurance nerd. People from my background rarely went to jail. I mean I was a Jewish Ph.D.

I was not from a street gang. I was a puny tax evader. But I was a contradiction. I was also a professional boxer, a rapper and now, my crowning glory, a felon.

My most consistent art was poetry. I was a real poet. My Ph.D. was in literature. I was gentle, polite and upper class. I was a gentleman. I was classy. But if you messed with me I would kill you. Or I thought I would. I was worried about rumors of gays attacking you in jail. No biggy to me. I'd kill them. No one touched me but me. I would masturbate when I got a free shower with a curtain. I was turned on by myself. I was disappointed by the rest of humanity.

A few months into my sentence two Dominicans sneaked out of the prison camp. There were no fences. It was easy to get away. But who would want to get away when at home most of us had no jobs and no futures? And if they caught you sneaking out you got eighteen months added onto your sentence. You didn't want to become a long termer because you'd be guaranteed no future on the outside. A two time loser is a schmuck who doesn't learn from experience.

I liked the structure of prison. It was a new life. A life imprisoned within its own daydreams. It was a step into another world.

The hacks were jigging their keys. I don't know why. They rarely locked someone up in solitary unless they put an inmate in for having a guest bring him dope or getting in a fight. The fights in Prison Camp weren't bad. Next door at the Medium Facility there were stabbings every other day. You'd know someone was stabbed when the siren went off and they closed the Medium Facility down. They'd send us back to our bunks even though we had nothing to do with the stabbings. There wasn't too much violence in the Prison Camp because we were all doing sentences of under ten years and we weren't anxious to compound our terms. In the Medium the average sentence was thirty years and they just didn't care if you added on to their sentences. These hard core criminals struck me as classless. I wouldn't stab anyone because I was afraid of getting a longer sentence but because it wasn't the right thing to do. Unless you messed with me. Then I'd kill you. It wasn't that I had a split personality. It's just that I was a fragmented rock in a rough ocean near an oil spill.

I remember going for a few walks on the quarter mile track with my codefendant Kelly. I didn't respect going for walks. During the day I would run six miles on the track. I was an athlete not a walker. Since we got in tax trouble I had discovered that Kelly was gay. I was worried that he would have an affair with another inmate and that the cons would think I was gay because we had worked together on the outside.

I'd tell him, "I don't want you messing around up here. No queer stuff. I don't want guilt by association."

"Don't worry boss," he said. For some reason I liked when he called me boss even though I was no longer even boss over myself. I was prison property. I was the hand in a handcuff. I didn't care. But the handcuff didn't exist. My being was in chains. I liked being trapped. You couldn't hurt me. I was tough. I was a man.

Actually Kelly hardly existed for me anymore. He was part of my past and in the past I didn't really know who he was. I didn't know that he was gay and in love with a transsexual, named Joseph. All I knew was that he placed a lot of insurance policies for my company. He was useful. He rang the cash register. I never new that he'd throw the cash register out the window.

The track under the stars was beautiful. It reminded me of when I used to walk around the Bois de Boulogne with my girlfriend (Lauren) before we got married,
when love was young and romance was foreign yet close.

I had a small desk in my cubicle that I shared with my current cellie. My mom would send me screen plays. I figured maybe I could get out of my poverty by writing movies. In fact I wrote my movie

"Suicide Club" in my cubicle. It later won the Angelika Film Festival and was published as a novel, "In the Suburb of Possible Suicide." I wrote nine other movies. I don't remember their names or what they were about. I also wrote a book of poems, "Steel Toe Boots." I worked out three hours a day. What could be more productive than jail? It was so much better than selling insurance. I could concentrate on writing and getting in shape for fighting.

I suppose I was a fiction of success. I no longer had my chauffeured Rolls Royce. I remember when I returned it to the dealership. It was on lease. The salesman said that I couldn't return it.

He took it when I told him I was going to jail. I gave him a ten thousand dollar tip because I didn't understand what it was to be broke with no prospects.

In the next cubicle to mine was a three hundred pound, six foot four tall drug dealer named Rockbottom. He looked like Baby Huey. He was a funny white guy.

All the black guys on the outside complain that the prison system is unfair to Blacks. They don't realize that the federal prison system is completely impartial. We don't even exist to the CO's. We are not human. They don't give a damn about skincolor. All they are interested in is our disclipline. We don't matter as long as we behave ourselves.

During my stay at Schuylkill Rocbottom's wife wrote him a Dear John. He laughed at the letter telling him she was leaving him for another guy. We don't care about much when we are in jail. We don't let the outside touch us. We are busy practicing solipsism and approximating Zen even though we don't attach official name tags to our games.

A big black weight lifter, George, dropped by and told me that he just bench pressed three hundred and fifty pounds. He said, "You don't want to mess with me." He's right.

Later I looked at my bunk mate, Billy. He wa always sleeping. I wonder if he thought that napping would shorten his ten year bid. I had planned to go into the drug business with Billy when I got out. He was a meth manufacturer in the Poconos. He told me if I knew a doctor in New York that could get a specific kind of ingredient that we could create a huge business.

I didn't know what else to do. I no longer had a business and I would need to make money. I knew just the right doctor who had money troubles and might strike a deal with us.

I was disappointed when Billie was moved to Allenwood. A couple of months later the warden called me into his office. This was the first time he wanted to speak to me. I was scared. He dropped his words on my plate in the non-perfunctory manner of all officials in the prison system. He said, "Billy is dead. He hung himself in solitary. I knew you were friendly with him so I'm telling you."

I thanked him for his candor. I didn't even know that I existed for him. I was just a number--03519-015. He generally ignored me. He nudged me to the door.

I didn't understand it. Billy seemed to go with the flow in jail. He only had five years of his ten-year sentence to go. His family often showed up on visiting day. I had heard that bikers controlled the meth business. Maybe one of them offed him. Maybe it wasn't suicide? Who knew? And when you got down to it, who really cared?

Life was cheap in jail. You didn't really realize it until one or more of your friends died. It was a graveyard waiting to happen either now or shortly after you got out.

One of my previous cellies, Nick, went home and overdosed on heroin. Here today gone tomorrow. I was just hanging in with a grin.

Paulie was my buddy from the Whitey Bulger gang. I used to run the track with him. Everybody, even the black guys, were scared of him. He was a good looking preppie guy. He could have been a high school quarterback. In fact, I think he was. I was glad to be his buddy. I figured if a fight broke out I could use him for protection.

Paulie was not the snitch type. Yet after about a year he told me that Whitey had promised his wife money and he wasn't paying her. He turned on Whitey and got out early in the Witness Protection Program. He moved to Florida and decided he didn't need any protection. He got in a fight at a bar and beat up an NFL football player. I lost track of him there.

They had a typing room with books in it at the camp. I only went there at night to type screenplays on these broken-down typewriters. This wasn't allowed in the typing library. You were only allowed to type legal briefs. Like the idiot prisoners would know how to handle their cases. The system favored morons. I was trying to write movie scripts and I had to sneak them past the guards.

When I was at Schuylkill I missed New York a bit. But I was also glad to be removed from my business problems and the feeling that I had failed my family. When I left for halfway house I remember standing out behind the dorm and feeling nostalgic. I cried a few tears. I had been through a dull adventure. I would miss it. I had done my time and flipped it on its head like a coin.

I hoped I could fit in at home. But I was offering nothing. I was a two-year convict rather than a high-powered business executive. I didn't want to start in insurance again at the bottom of the pile. I didn't have energy to climb up from failure. I had the urge to wallow in what I had become rather than lift myself up on the ladder of ambition.

AFTERWORD

My book, *The Displaced Chunks of My Life: A Memoir,* is a book of autobiographical stories and some personal essays. I have a surprisingly variegated, complex life and the stories break it down into energetic fragments. I have always felt that I am special. Maybe I have delusions of grandeur? Maybe I am grander than my delusions?

I have been a ranked ski racer, ranked tennis player and ranked professional boxer.

I have a Ph.D. and have been a CEO. When I was in my twenties I taught English at Hunter College, Herbert Lehman College, Keene College and LaGuardia College. Then I went into my father's insurance business and became a big success. I became modestly rich.

Magazines that featured me are *People Magazine, New York Magazine, Men's Journal, Time Out Magazine, Men's Journal, Stern Magazine and newspapers such as Wall Street Journal, The New York Times, The Post, the Daily News,* etc., etc. I have been interviewed on television, including the *Phil Donahue Show.* I don't know how many radio shows, including Hot 97.

My published poetry books are *Living on Madison Avenue* (Future Cycle Press), *Lane Changes (*Four Way Books) and *Dementia Pugilistica, (Turtle* Bay Press). I have also published *Blame it on the Scientists* (Poetry Chapbook), and two memoirs, *The King* of *White Collar Boxing (*Rain Mountain *Press), Jail*: *The Essays* (Prison Foundation).

I have published a thousand poems in many of the journals. My novel, *In the Suburb of Possible Suicide* was published by Adelaide Press in 2020. And another book of my poems—*Broken Paragraphs*—is being published in the UK by Eyewear Books in 2001.

This manuscript is my collection of memoirs and essays. I am temporarily larger than my works. Hopefully, my writings will be recognized as larger than me. So much to do about size and longevity. Who cares? I do. I don't. The congruity of contradiction runs like my life's stream.

www.ingramcontent.com/pod-product-compliance
Lightning Source LLC
LaVergne TN
LVHW090929150826
845672LV00006B/1452

* 9 7 8 9 3 6 3 5 4 9 7 5 3 *